Allergan's First Fifty Years

Harrison Stephens and Nancy Fries

Greenwich Publishing Group, Inc.
Lyme, Connecticut

AF817112

Dedication

On the occasion of Allergan's 50th anniversary — January 27, 2000 — this volume tells the remarkable story of the beginning of our company. It is a story about the vision that fueled Allergan's emergence. But more than that, it's about the people who made it possible: our employees, physicians, investors and customers, all of whom lifted us to where we are today.

As with all entrepreneurial efforts, nothing is more important than the quality of the individuals who contributed so much to what we have achieved. Bright, dedicated and energetic employees repeatedly made the commitment to stimulate the excellence that has been critical to our building the reputation that we enjoy.

What is embedded deeply in our company's history, and in the determination of each member of our organization past and present, is the knowledge that listening to our customers is what drives our progress. Focusing on our customers' needs, and in turn the greater health that grows from that focus, is what sets us apart.

We view the future with great anticipation and excitement. We see prospects in the next century for the development and growth of products which not only make our business a success but are recognized globally for their contribution to the wellbeing of families.

Setting our goals high is an Allergan tradition. Achieving them is what we strive for, and we hope this book invites you better to understand our exceptional past and how we will build on it.

Gavin Herbert
Chairman Emeritus and Founder

David Pyott
President and Chief Executive Officer

50 Allergan's First Fifty Years

Harrison Stephens and Nancy Fries

GREENWICH PUBLISHING GROUP, INC.
LYME, CONNECTICUT

©2000 Allergan, Inc. All rights reserved.

Printed and bound in the United States of America. No part of this publication may be reproduced or transmitted in any form or by any means, electronic or mechanical, including photocopying, recording or any information storage and retrieval system now known or to be invented, without permission in writing from Allergan, Inc., Corporate Communications, 2525 DuPont Drive, P.O. Box 19534, Irvine, CA 92623-6751, except by a reviewer who wishes to quote brief passages in connection with a review written for inclusion in a magazine, newspaper or broadcast.

Produced and published by Greenwich Publishing Group, Inc.
Lyme, Connecticut

Design by Clare Cunningham Graphic Design

Separation and film assembly by Scan Communications Group, Inc.

Library of Congress Card Number: 99-069256

ISBN: 0-944641-40-7

First Printing: January 2000

10 9 8 7 6 5 4 3 2 1

The following are registered trademarks of companies indicated:
Accutane — Roche
Retin A — Johnson & Johnson
Tagamet — SmithKline
Xalatan — Pharmacia & Upjohn, Inc.

TRADEMARKS
All product names appearing in this book are trademarks or service marks that are owned by, licensed to, promoted by, or distributed by Allergan, Inc., its subsidiaries or affiliates.

Acular[1], Allergan, (antihistamine eye drop), Allergan (nasal drop) Allergan Soaking Solution, Alphagan, AMO Diplomax, AMO Phacoflex II, AMO Prestige, Array, Azelex, Betagan, Blephamide, Blink-N-Clean, Botox, Complete brand, Consept F, Cortefrin, Epifrin, FML Liquifilm, Herplex, HydroCare, Lens Plus, Liquifilm Liquifilm Tears, Liquifilm Wetting Solution, LC65 Cleaning Solution, MD Forte, Oculfox, Prednefrin, Prefrin, Propine, Restasis, Sensar, Soflens, Sovereign, Tazoract, The Unfolder and Zorac.

[1]Acular is a registered trademark licensed from Syntex (U.S.A.) Inc.

photo on previous pages: Celebrations have always been a part of Allergan's culture. In the late 1960s, the company purchased former farming property in Irvine, California. With shovel in hand, Gavin Herbert Jr. turned the first soil at a company-wide groundbreaking ceremony for what was to become Tower 1.

ACKNOWLEDGEMENTS

This book would not have been possible without the time and attention scores of Allergan employees and friends have generously given the project throughout the research and interviewing process. Special thanks go to Stephanie Duver, Carol Dykes, Jolene Jennings, Gary Lu and Hasani Deziaueto for their dilligence in finding the perfect picture and good humor managing the myriad details that a book like this entails.

Table of Contents

STOCKHOLM
GOTHENBURG
DUBLIN
COPENHAGEN
HORSENS
GLASGOW
BIRMINGHAM
SOUTHAMPTON
NEWCASTLE
LONDON
BRISTOL
UTRECHT
WATFORD
NOTTINGHAM
CARDIFF
MANCHESTER
ANTWERP
HAMBURG
MÜNSTER
BREMEN
BERLIN
ESSEN
HANNOVER
KÖLN
KASSEL
MAGDEBURG
LEIPZIG
WIESBADEN
WEIMAR
WÜRZBURG
BEXBACH
REUTLINGEN
NÜRNBERG
MÜNCHEN
LILLE
STRASBOURG
BREST
PARIS
METZ
LINZ
NANTES
CLERMONT-FERRAND
ZURICH
RENNES
TOURS
ROUEN
DIJON
GRENOBLE
POITIERS
LYON
LAUSANNE
PORTO
BORDEAUX
LIMOGES
NICE
TOULOUSE
TOULON
LISBON
MONTPELLIER
MARSEILLE
LECCE
GENOVA
TORINO
BARCELONA
ANCONA
VALENCIA
CAGLIARI
ROMA
PESCARA
OVIEDO
MADRID
VERONA
FERRARA
NAPOLI
PARMA
SEVILLA
ZARAGOZA
MURCIA
UDINE
PALERMO
MESSINA
MALAGA

1 The New Allergan

It is the spirit of the men who follow and of the man who leads that gains the victory. — George Smith Patton

At age 25, Gavin Shearer Herbert Jr. took over the tiny company his father had started. He found niches in the pharmaceutical industry his firm could fill and built the company into a corporation respected all over the world. Its principal business from the beginning has been eye-care products, and there probably isn't an ophthalmologist in the world who isn't familiar with the name Allergan. But some of the zest that had built Allergan from a drugstore annex into a billion-dollar-a-year pharmaceutical company drifted in the mid-1990s.

Alphagan® (brimonidine tartrate ophthalmic solution) 0.2%

On October 26, 1999, Allergan staged the Pan-European Glaucoma Symposium, a live video transmission from Orlando, Florida, to 100 cities throughout Europe. With simultaneous translation into four languages, the event reached almost 6,000 ophthalmologists. A presentation on the clinical efficacy and safety of Alphagan was the highlight of the event.

The chief executive officer knew it. The board of directors knew it. Wall Street knew it — the stock price stayed flat. Gusto, spirit, enthusiasm, elan — whatever it's called — is elusive. William C. Shepherd, the CEO who had, as he put it, "blessed every decision for 14 years," decided a new chief might find it. He asked to be replaced as head of the Irvine, California-based company, and he led the search for his successor.

David E. I. Pyott succeeded Bill Shepherd as CEO in January of 1998 and immediately began a transformation of the company. A year and a half later, Allergan's stock price was up threefold, its product sales were approaching $1.5 billion a year and a sense of excitement permeated the whole organization worldwide.

David Pyott arrived at Allergan in January 1998 and started a successful transformation of the company, returning it to its historic roots of being fast, lean and very responsive to customers' needs. Due to sales success of recently introduced products such as Alphagan, Tazorac and Array, the company posted a 13.3 percent gain in sales at constant currency rates. The market responded by boosting its share price threefold during 1998 and 1999.

"I called it a journey back into the future," Pyott says, "because I felt I was returning the company in many ways to the very entrepreneurial phase that had existed under Gavin's leadership.

"When I started here and assessed the culture, I felt there were strong entrepreneurial roots going back all the way to the founding fathers, the Herberts," Pyott says. "But I think there were also aspects of large pharmaceutical bureaucracy. One of the questions I asked myself was, 'How do we just scrub off the layer of silt and mud lying on the sound pilings of the company and go back down to the real, strong genetic roots?' That was all part of instilling the attitude that we're not a big company; we had to return to the attitude of fast and small and being responsive to, above all, our customers. That was really the starting point."

Letting the Stars Shine

The first objective for the new CEO was "a crystal clear strategy," Pyott says. He credits the firm's middle managers rather than himself for developing it. ("When I arrived, I couldn't even spell ophthalmology," he jokes.) He hired a consulting firm, McKinsey & Company, to help develop what he called a strategic reformulation. He entrusted the middle managers with the task of developing the strategy, appointing one work group for each of Allergan's businesses: ophthalmic pharmaceuticals, surgical, contact-lens care, dermatology and neuromuscular. Each work group's suggestions went to a steering committee, then to the executive committee of senior managers, known as ECom, and finally to the board.

"That wasn't the way planning had been done in the organization," says Lynn Dorsey Bleil, who led the McKinsey team. "He selected the best and the brightest — who could bring good energy and great ideas to the table — and provided a vehicle by which they were going to get a lot of visibility with senior management. They'd get exposure and be on the hook for sending and pushing forward these creative ideas."

Pyott found that some regions were mixing together all the various businesses, when each has different requirements for research and development as well as different product life cycles. The new strategy was to get people focused on the needs of each separate business. To carry it out, Pyott had to create a new organization. He "turned the organization on its head" by decentralizing all the operations. "About nine months after my arrival, people understood that progress wasn't a voluntary program; everybody had to be part of the progress," says Pyott. "And they were, with almost no exception. I think one of the happiest parts of the new organization is how few people were asked to leave, which in turn corroborated the excellence of the 'genetic material' here — a great culture and super people."

The New Allergan

"David started to use the phrase 'The New Allergan' in his presentations to the broader organization," Dorsey Bleil says, "and then began to use it more in his internal and external communications. And it seemed to play well and be quite fitting for a whole host of new changes: new strategies for each of the product lines, a new organization, a new culture, a new way of doing things and a new mentality. It encompassed the broad range of things that were, if you will, 'new' about the organization."

The turnaround of the skin-care business demonstrates how the New Allergan's strategy allows each business area to contribute to the bottom line. Tazorac, a pharmaceutical to treat psoriasis, was the first product Allergan developed from inventing the molecule to marketing the product, a years-long process. Expectations were high: probably an over-$100 million product. Year-three initial sales hit about one-tenth of that projection.

"There was a strategy to try and sell this product ourselves everywhere," Pyott says. "We were a one-product company (in the skin-care field) outside North America. How could we make money? We were definitely struggling in this business. The first thing we did was retrench. We out-licensed Tazorac for markets outside the U.S. to strong dermatology partners. We expect a nice royalty stream from these partners — a very high percentage of their sales. That money then goes back into our U.S. marketing."

But while Allergan licensed overseas sales to companies already in the field, the firm added money for research and development of the product, expanding indications and financing studies of comparing Tazorac to other products in the field. "The results can then be presented as scientific papers at conventions," Pyott continues, "and from those we can derive abstracts and selling pieces for the sales force. And our second product, Azelex for acne, which had been suffering in the shadow of the big product, is also up in prescriptions. The good news is that our skin-care business is strong and growing. Management now understands that even if it's tough, we're here to stay and we're here to win."

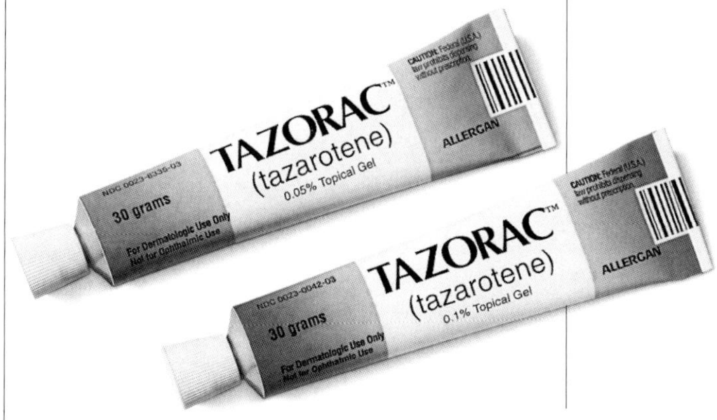

Allergan's new psoriasis gel is named Zorac globally, with the exception of the U.S. and Canada, where it is named Tazorac. It is the first product the company developed from molecule to market, and its worldwide acceptance led to a turnaround in Allergan's dermatology business.

Tough Decisions

The emergence of the New Allergan was not without pain. To create it, Pyott initiated a variety of strategic moves that a local California business publication summed up as "Less Fat, More Brains." In September 1998, Allergan announced plans to streamline operations and reduce costs through restructuring and plant consolidations. By 2001, restructuring is predicted to save the company $22 million compared to 1998 expenses. Plant consolidations are predicted to save another $13 million. The savings are being achieved, in part, by cutting 550 jobs over a three-year period.

Coming just months after Pyott joined the company, the decision sparked criticism of the new CEO and some longings for the old Allergan. "It would be incorrect to say there weren't wounds," Pyott concedes. But saving money wasn't his only motivation: "I wanted to save the money to recycle it back into R&D and sales forces and marketing programs, and I didn't want to be the leader of the kind of company that would be slow and lumbering and unresponsive to customers." By the end of 1998, the global sales force had been expanded by more than 10 percent. "People began to understand that this wasn't just rhetoric," Pyott says. "This was fact and action." Board member Henry Wendt (who is a blue-water sailor) said of the early months of the transformation, "It was tough, and we went through some choppy water, but the sails are trimmed beautifully now, and this vessel is moving hard on the wind."

"They've got great talent in the organization," Dorsey Bleil says. "And they have a mindset that is so very different than the one they had a year ago. They now believe in themselves and they believe they can do things. They are gaining confidence with more aggressive, bold moves and more risk-taking. That is exactly what is going to be needed to navigate the rapidly evolving biopharmaceutical landscape."

Pyott's "understated leadership style" is one reason for this change in attitude, according to Dorsey Bleil. "David is a very hands-on person. He spends lots of time on the road. He gets involved in the details,

Pyott's "New Allergan" means saving money wherever possible and plowing large portions of it into R&D, the lifeblood of any pharmaceutical company. Successful products like Tazorac/Zorac that Allergan has developed from molecule to market in-house place added emphasis on the R&D operation.

which (particularly in this case) is critical to making the right decisions and energizing people — instilling the feeling that this is a different day. He's also very tough. He sets very aggressive targets and lets everyone know that they are going to be met. He is also a very good listener…and he's responsive. He can get into a good, heated debate when he has a different opinion. But he's very open minded."

Before coming to Allergan, Pyott was head of the nutrition division and a member of the executive committee of Novartis AG. "This was a big step for him," Dorsey Bleil says. "It was a very big change and I think a very energizing opportunity — one that was pretty high-stakes. He has grown significantly as a leader and he has a tremendous amount of perspective. Not just because he's in the seat of power, but because of what he knows and what he does."

Board member Handel Evans, who is a consultant to the pharmaceutical industry, says Pyott provided "a breath of fresh air." Gavin Herbert, now chairman emeritus, agrees. "I'm very pleased with a renewed spirit, an entrepreneurial attitude," he says. "I think we'd gotten a bit too bureaucratic and slow in making decisions." Frank Tunney, corporate vice president of administration, general counsel and secretary, says, "The New Allergan has a renewed external focus on customers and markets and a renewed appreciation of the importance of fast, flexible responsiveness to their needs."

Dancing Between Their Feet

As a relatively small entity, Allergan can be a fierce competitor to the pharmaceutical giants. "We know what we're doing so well," Pyott says, "that we can dance between their feet while they're still trying to work out what's moving down there on the ground."

A key to keeping Allergan so nimble is breaking assignments down into manageable pieces and leaving them in the hands of small, fast teams, where the experts are formulating plans. Pyott favors a team size of about seven people. When a team puts together a plan, it goes up the chain of command quickly, often by phone, voice mail or e-mail. If a plan requires Pyott's approval or support, he tries to provide it within hours. "I may come back on the computer with a few clarification questions," he says, "and then we do it. And because of the quality of the people here, the preparation has gotten better and better. So I have fewer questions. Now it's usually, 'Looks great. Get going.' We've become very quick in the marketplace."

Not surprisingly, Pyott is confident of Allergan's growth and its ability to remain agile by continuing to "break down the

Opposite, fast, flexible teams have been the hallmark of the New Allergan. Groups of about seven seem to spark the best entrepreneurial ideas, according to Pyott. Above, from whatever angle one views Allergan's Irvine headquarters, there is a sense of stability, excitement, self-confidence and untapped growth potential being unleashed.

pile" into small, autonomous units. "I see sustainable growth trending toward 15 percent annual sales growth in local currency," he says. "As an objective, we see in the coming years 20 percent earnings-per-share growth."

Allergan's recently recruited chief financial officer, Eric Brandt, agrees. "You can look at the company and see that it's pretty likely to double in size over the next four years or so," Brandt says. "I think that was one of the aspirations I had in coming here." Brandt was a senior member of the health-care practice unit in the distinguished Boston Consulting Group before Pyott persuaded him to join Allergan in May of 1999. To do so, Brandt turned down offers from several pharmaceutical giants.

"To have a role as a chief financial officer, to have a duty to insure the financial integrity and to be a partner with David — helping to think through some of the more strategic issues facing the business and leverage off knowledge and experience from other places — I felt was a tremendously exciting and challenging opportunity, and something that certainly would not be boring. Judging by the number of new things that pop up on my desk every day, it's definitely not boring."

Brandt believes Allergan "is at a cusp right now. It is a business that is performing extremely well. I think we're in a position of strength." Dorsey Bleil agrees: "Their prospects are bright. The market is rewarding them. That gives them good flexibility as well to make some creative, bold moves. But most importantly, their people are feeling good, and they're able to continue to attract great talent, which is going to be critical going forward. They went through quite a dramatic change in the last year and a half. I think having a sense of the history and the company's roots and how far they've come can be very energizing."

And what of the old Allergan — the drugstore loft where the first Allergan products were formulated half a century ago? Allergan headquarters in Irvine is only 40 miles from that site, but the distance between the expectations of that time and the realities of today is beyond measure. On the pages that follow is the story of that journey.

2 Startup

Look with favor upon a bold beginning. — Virgil

LOS ANGELES PHARMACIST GAVIN S. HERBERT SR. WAS INTENT ON DEVELOPING A CHAIN OF DRUGSTORES. HE HAD STARTED HIS OWN PHARMACY AT LOS ANGELES'S WILSHIRE BOULEVARD AND ST. ANDREWS PLACE IN 1945 AND HAD A PROFITABLE BUSINESS. BUT WHEN HIS FRIEND, CHEMIST STANLEY BLY, APPROACHED HIM WITH AN IDEA IN 1949, HIS INTEREST AND HIS ENTREPRENEURIAL INSTINCT WERE IGNITED. BLY HAD AN IDEA FOR A NEW KIND OF ANTI-ALLERGY NOSE DROP, AND HERBERT HAD THE MEANS AND SAVVY TO BRING IT TO MARKET. THEY CALLED IT "ALLERGAN."

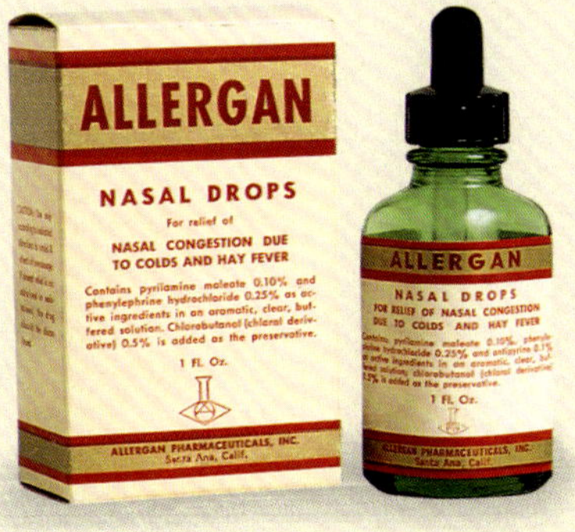

It was the father-son team of Gavin Herbert Sr. and Jr., seen here in a 1970s photo, who were Allergan's first visionaries: Gavin Sr. for having the idea to market anti-allergy nasal drops bearing the Allergan name, and Gavin Jr. for building the company into today's research and marketing powerhouse.

Gavin Herbert Sr., right, was a true entrepreneur. He not only built a profitable chain of drugstores but also launched a venture that would one day be known as Allergan. Joined by Stanley Bly, a chemist friend, Herbert and his son Gavin Jr. mixed product batches in the balcony of the pharmacy, on the ground floor of the Wilshire professional building, below. The pharmacy, far right, can be seen to the left of the large, center door in the photo below. The building was filled with the offices of physicians, including several ophthalmologists who provided helpful advice to the young enterprise.

The name derived from the words "allergy" and "neoantergan," a principal ingredient. They set up a small laboratory in the balcony of the drugstore to make the solution and create other products. Herbert's teenage son, Gavin Jr., helped his father in the drugstore after school and was fascinated with the activity on the balcony. Gavin remembers that some product batches were so small "you could mix them in a quart bottle."

This was not Herbert Sr.'s first venture. In addition to the pharmacy, he had started a small business the year before with pediatrician Alonzo Cass, who had an idea for a solution to stop thumb sucking. "The product was just not a good idea," Gavin Jr. said years later. "Fortunately, they abandoned the product before spending money trying to sell it." But the men had already incorporated the business as Child Institute, Inc. It was a paper corporation with nothing but a name — the perfect corporate shell for Herbert Sr. and Bly's new enterprise. On January 27, 1950, Herbert simply renamed it Allergan Pharmaceuticals, Inc., and later that year introduced the nasal drop to the Los Angeles market.

A creative ophthalmologist and friend suggested to Herbert and Bly that they reformulate the product as an eye drop to treat allergic conjunctivitis, a pesky inflammation of the eye. As would be repeated time and time again over the next 50 years, the company opened the door to success by responding to the suggestion of a customer. The new formulation, introduced in 1952, was the first antihistamine eye drop in the United States. It worked well, and sales to Los Angeles ophthalmologists were brisk.

That was the birth of today's billion-dollar Allergan, Inc., but its later stature was not immediately apparent: Allergan's income tax return for 1950 listed gross sales of $4,187.88. Gross profits were $1,679.89, and after deductions, the company showed a loss of $2,424.68.

By that time, young Gavin had enrolled in pre-pharmacy courses at the University of Southern California (USC), but he still came into the pharmacy to help. "Stan Bly was the one who had product ideas," Gavin remembers. "He had a creative mind. I found it more interesting to work with him in the lab than to count pills, type labels and dust bottles in the drugstore."

Bright Young Minds

In 1953, Herbert Sr. recruited John Biles, a young USC teacher with a Ph.D. in chemistry, as a part-time consultant to the Allergan lab on Thursday afternoons and Saturday mornings. He worked with Bly in developing Cortefrin, the first cortisone eye drop, to treat allergic inflammation. "Working at Allergan was exciting," Biles recalls. "I could hardly wait to get there. There was something different every day. The first year I worked with them, our total gross sales for the year were $25,000. I remember one day

By 1953, the company had moved into a larger, adjacent balcony to produce Allergan eye drops as well as formulate new products, such as Cortefrin, the first cortisone eye drop, and Prednefrin, one of the first ophthalmic steroid decongestants on the market. With the help of a part-time pharmacy professor, John Biles, and a full-time salesman, Glenn Pughe, the fledgling company was ready to spread its wings.

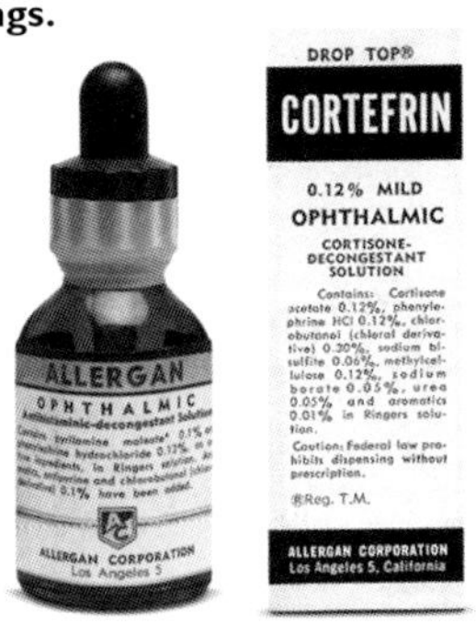

when we had orders that totaled $320 and we celebrated."

Biles continued his part-time relationship with Allergan until 1968, when he became dean of the School of Pharmacy at USC. He remained on the Allergan board for another dozen years. "I'd say Allergan was one of the two or three professional experiences that rank at the top for me," he said recently.

The men worked on several other eye-care products, including Cortefrin, and soon Allergan hired its first salesman, Glenn Pughe. He, Bly and the Herberts all made regular visits to doctors' offices promoting their products to ophthalmologists. (Gavin remembers being asked to leave one doctor's office because he didn't know enough about the pharmacology of the formulations.)

A few months after starting at Allergan, Biles saved the company from demise. Chemist Stanley Bly was both brilliant and insecure, according to Biles, and "did not share the core product formulas with anybody. Then he died suddenly. So I had to reconstitute the formulas." In the days before computerized chemical analysis equipment, it took lots of trial and error before Biles's new formulations perfectly matched Bly's original ones, but ultimately he succeeded.

In 1953 the lab moved across the hall into an adjacent balcony that was somewhat larger. At about that time, the U.S. Food and Drug Administration (FDA) decreed that all ophthalmic preparations had to be sterile. An organism called pseudomonas had turned up in other non-sterile ophthalmic preparations, blinding some users.

The new regulation ended most drugstore formulations, as pharmacists generally did not have the equipment to produce sterile formulations. Biles created that capability for Allergan, but it wasn't easy. A sterile environment had to be made in the little lab, containers had to be sterilized with steam, and products were put through microfilters. For Allergan, the change became an opportunity for growth as the need for sterile products emerged.

Rising to the Call

In 1953, Gavin Jr. was drafted into the Navy and assigned to the pharmacy at the San Diego Naval Hospital. The same year, Gavin Sr. was seriously injured in an auto accident, and for several months Allergan drifted without a rudder. However, the younger Herbert spent his spare moments trying to keep the business going. He drove to the store about twice a month to help out. In the late afternoons when he wasn't on Navy duty, he called on San Diego doctors, and sales continued to increase.

This period helped Gavin Jr. make a critical choice about the direction his life would take. During his stint as a Navy pharmacist, Gavin had his fill of pharmacy operations, and he knew a future in retail was not going to satisfy him. The lure of the blossoming Allergan business, however, was very powerful. When he was mustered out of the Navy in 1957, Gavin and his father had some soul-searching conversations.

"My father's main interest was the drugstores," Gavin says, "and he really didn't see much future in Allergan. Dad felt that Allergan would never grow the way the drugstore business would, and he wanted to devote his time and energies to what he knew best." As John Biles remembers it, at one point in the 1950s, the elder Herbert would have sold the company for $50,000, but his son persuaded him not to.

"In a way, Dad's doubts were a big stimulant for me," says Gavin. "I don't remember specifically whether it was because of my age and the feeling that I could do anything, or whether it had something to do with my wanting to prove he was wrong. Dad never really felt Allergan could compete with the likes of Upjohn, Merck and other established specialty companies like Alcon. He told me to forget this 'impossible dream.' The more he talked like that, the more determined I was to make it succeed. Having a chance to run a business — even a tiny one — was a heady experience for me, and I was determined to succeed."

The Young President

The founder of a successful business is usually the dynamo who builds on that success. But when his father gave up directing Allergan, Gavin Jr. became the engine that drove the business.

The 25-year-old, untried president of a company with about $100,000 a year in sales examined his qualifications for the job. "It was pretty evident that I had little or no background or knowledge in any of the key areas that would create a successful company," Gavin says. "So I began recruiting part-time specialists in half a dozen areas in pharmaceutical sales and marketing and some areas of product development. We put together the team slowly and later had full-time people. That was the first time there was any kind of concerted management effort to build the company."

"He surrounded himself with people who could be very helpful to him," recalls

Thomas E. "Ed" O'Sullivan, the Herbert family lawyer and Allergan board member for many years. "His management style was very hands-on, and he sought advice from people he thought would have sound advice. That's one of his great strengths. He may not do what you tell him," O'Sullivan chuckles, "but he will listen. Gavin was very creative, and when he came into the business, he was the driving force."

One of the people whose expertise Gavin immediately sought was Jack Browning, a pharmaceutical marketing executive working for the Robert Wilson Agency, a New York City firm specializing in medical advertising. Browning had previously worked at a major pharmaceutical company, SmithKline & French. Gavin thought it was time to begin selling Allergan products nationally and wanted Browning's marketing savvy. Browning flew to California on weekends to work on the marketing campaign. He and Gavin chose Prednefrin, one of about a half-dozen Allergan products, for national promotion.

Prednefrin was one of the first ophthalmic steroid decongestants on the market and was effective in treating eye inflammation. It was a good candidate for national promotion. Allergan couldn't afford a national sales force, but Browning worked out a mailing campaign targeting the nation's ophthalmologists with 18 or 20 mailings over a year. The men agreed it would take an expenditure in the $25,000 range to launch the promotion — more than Allergan's entire annual promotional budget.

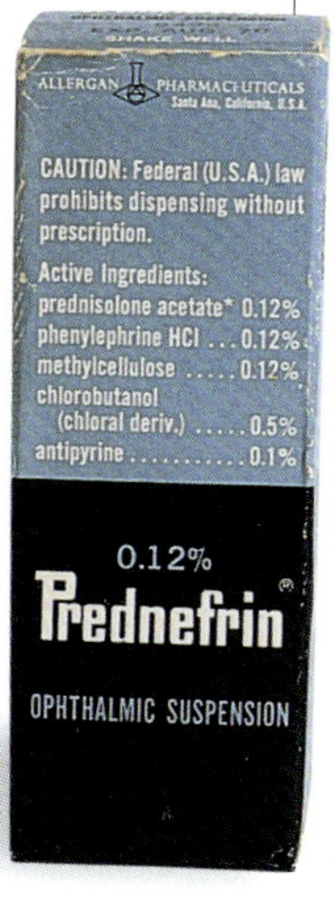

Gavin remembers approaching a banker who had worked with the company in the past. "He explained to me that we were technically bankrupt," Gavin says. "But he did loan me the $25,000 because he believed in the concept and thought the product introduction would be successful."

Browning devised an Allergan logo and designed a letterhead, labels and other printed materials to build a "progressively conservative" image of the company. He placed ads in a few ophthalmic journals. The campaign was effective, and Allergan began gaining recognition as a small national supplier of ophthalmic pharmaceuticals. "I wrote most of the promotional material they produced for the next 10 years or so," Browning says. He left New York, had his own promotional agency in Pasadena, California, for several years and eventually joined Allergan full time.

Gavin had completed three years of college as a pre-pharmacy major before he was drafted into the Navy. After the service and following his decision to return to Allergan, he re-enrolled at USC as a part-time student, changed his major to marketing and completed his degree — all while running the company. His father, although spending most of his time building a chain of drugstores, retained his title as chairman of the Allergan board. According to Gavin, "My father was a great salesman. He had a lot of good ideas and contacts that contributed to the growth of the company."

Listening to New Ideas

Gavin was always open to ideas from without as well as within. One came from Orville Miller, a pharmacologist at USC

Prednefrin, a treatment for eye inflammation, was the first Allergan product to be marketed nationally. Steroid decongestants were relatively new to the market, and Allergan's national advertisements distinguished Prednefrin from similar products by billing it as a mild steroid that could be used for longer periods of time using the analogy of "the ocular powderpuff."

who had studied Native American herbal medicine. One of the tribal medications he'd learned about was the use of dried rattlesnake meat to cure severe ocular allergies. Gavin continues the story:

"He interested a very well-known ophthalmologist in testing this stuff. So we took 20 pounds of rattlesnake meat to the USC pharmacy school to process it. It was over a weekend. I guess it was supposed to be refrigerated and wasn't. So this terrible odor began coming from one of the pharmacy labs. One of the custodians thought there'd been a murder and called the police.

"Actually, the product was tested over two or three years and appeared to have some efficacy, but we could never figure out which of the components of rattlesnake meat were the beneficial ingredients; ultimately, we gave up."

Despite its early problems, Allergan had been modestly profitable from its second year on, and the 1,000-square-foot lab was soon inadequate. In 1957, when Gavin Jr. took charge, he decided to move the company into an old theater the police vice squad had closed down for staging X-rated plays. The Halliburton family, owners of the building, turned it into a laboratory for Allergan. Gavin's office was just off the lobby. The floor where the seats had been became the production, packaging and labeling area and a sterile filling area was set up in the former projection booth. Storage was in the balcony and on the stage.

Around the same time, Gavin hired Malcolm Boghosian, a highly creative young pharmacist fresh from USC, to develop products. Boghosian coupled a solid grounding in pharmaceuticals with a Thomas Edison approach to invention: Try a lot of things until you find something that works.

By then, Gavin had decided to establish a niche for the company in a pharmaceutical industry dominated by giants. Allergan's business would be eye care. He assigned Boghosian the job of developing products in the field of ophthalmology.

Herbert turned his own shortage of knowledge in the field of ophthalmology into an asset that still serves the company well: the rare art of listening. He and Boghosian regularly called on ophthalmologists to find out what they needed, what diseases had inadequate medications, what chemicals might be formulated into a solution to treat a particular condition and what advances in ophthalmology were likely. Every Allergan executive through the years has followed that practice.

Out of one of those meetings came the idea of using sulfacetamide and a steroid in a formulation to attack blepharitis, a stubbornly persistent infection of the eyelid. Ointments in use at the time were not particularly effective.

In working on the blepharitis drug, Boghosian tried several solutions that didn't work out. "We were hunting and hunting," he says. Then he made an important connection. Boghosian had developed several earlier products, including a solution to clean and lubricate contact lenses. It contained 2 percent polyvinyl alcohol (PVA), which forms a thin, transparent film. "I wondered if the lens-wetting solution would act as a vehicle for the medication," he recalls. It did; the film held the medication in the eye longer than anything else he'd tried.

Boghosian employed his Edison approach to determine the exact percentage of PVA for the product. "I remember trying several concentrations in my own eye," he

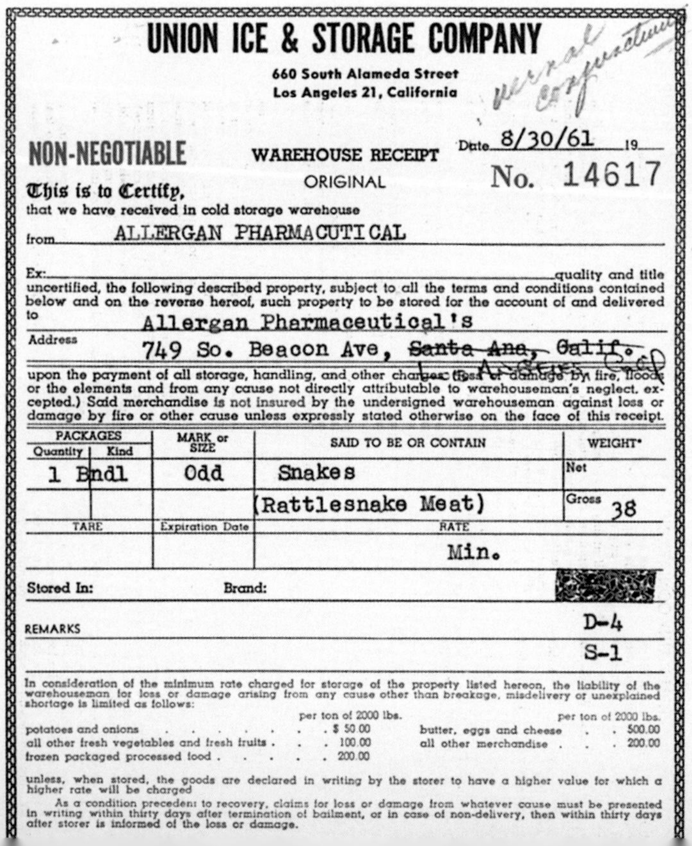
UNION ICE & STORAGE COMPANY
660 South Alameda Street
Los Angeles 21, California

NON-NEGOTIABLE WAREHOUSE RECEIPT ORIGINAL

Date 8/30/61 19

No. 14617

This is to Certify, that we have received in cold storage warehouse

from ALLERGAN PHARMACUTICAL

Ex: quality and title uncertified, the following described property, subject to all the terms and conditions contained below and on the reverse hereof, such property to be stored for the account of and delivered to Allergan Pharmaceutical's

Address 749 So. Beacon Ave, ~~Santa Ana,~~ Calif.

upon the payment of all storage, handling, and other charges (loss or damage by fire, floods or the elements and from any cause not directly attributable to warehouseman's neglect, excepted.) Said merchandise is not insured by the undersigned warehouseman against loss or damage by fire or other cause unless expressly stated otherwise on the face of this receipt.

PACKAGES Quantity	Kind	MARK or SIZE	SAID TO BE OR CONTAIN	WEIGHT*
1	Bndl	Odd	Snakes	Net
			(Rattlesnake Meat)	Gross 38
TARE		Expiration Date	RATE	
			Min.	

Stored In: Brand: [redacted]

REMARKS D-4 S-1

In consideration of the minimum rate charged for storage of the property listed hereon, the liability of the warehouseman for loss or damage arising from any cause other than breakage, misdelivery or unexplained shortage is limited as follows:

	per ton of 2000 lbs.		per ton of 2000 lbs.
potatoes and onions	$ 50.00	butter, eggs and cheese	500.00
all other fresh vegetables and fresh fruits	100.00	all other merchandise	200.00
frozen packaged processed food	200.00		

unless, when stored, the goods are declared in writing by the storer to have a higher value for which a higher rate will be charged

As a condition precedent to recovery, claims for loss or damage from whatever cause must be presented in writing within thirty days after termination of bailment, or in case of non-delivery, then within thirty days after storer is informed of the loss or damage.

From the first, Allergan's success was built on listening to ideas from customers and from the scientific community. One pharmacologist even convinced Gavin Herbert Jr. to test rattlesnake meat as a cure for severe ocular allergies, as the bill at left confirms.

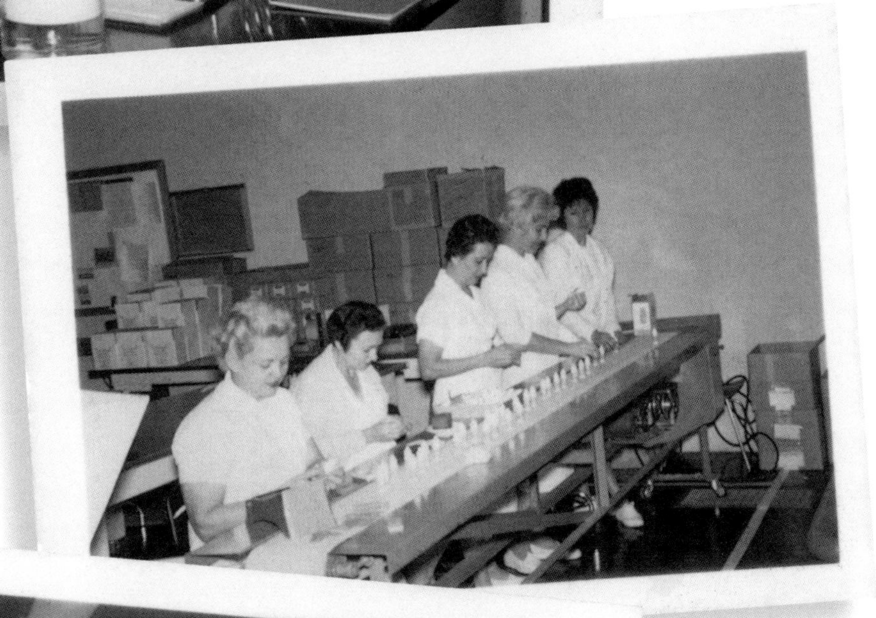

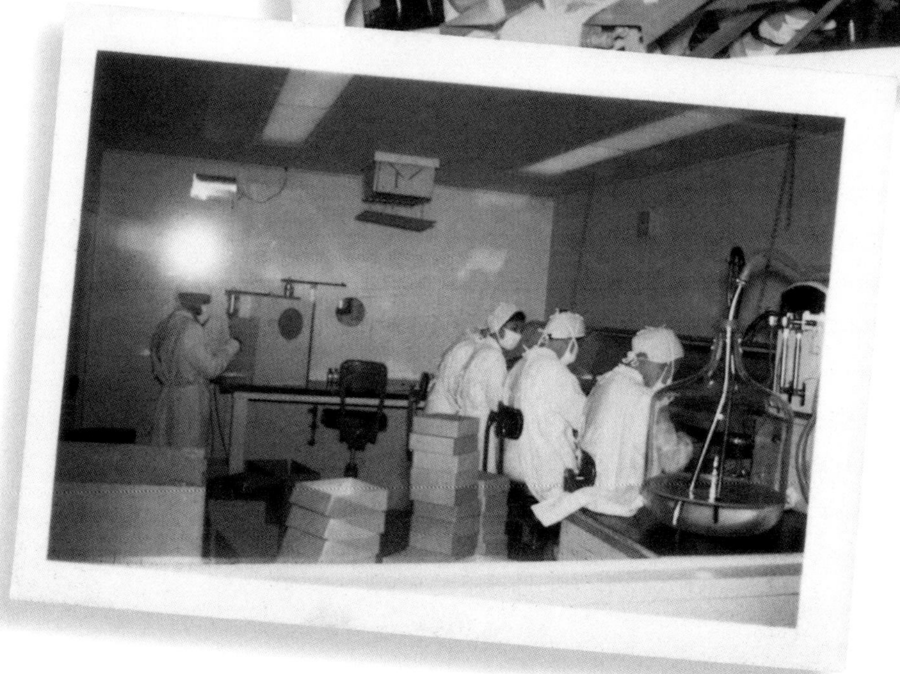

In 1957, the young president of Allergan, Gavin Herbert Jr., moved the company to the Halliburton Building in downtown Los Angeles. The Halliburton family, owners of the Halliburton Company with offices in the same building, converted what was once the X-rated Beaux Arts Theater into offices, labs and production facilities for Allergan. These pictures depict early Allergan employees mixing the product, hand assembling, and manning the sterile filling line in what had been the projection booth.

Gavin Herbert Jr. — Not Just the Boss

Gavin Herbert is a big man, well over six feet tall, respected within the halls of Allergan and the industry. His sometimes demanding manner is leavened by a sense of humor and an almost boyish grin.

Gavin can appreciate a gag, even when it's on him. At an employee carnival he once volunteered as a target for a cream pie-throwing contest.

In another instance, Dave Saylor, a long-time sales leader of the company, decided to get even with Gavin about a ribbing he'd taken. He borrowed a female mannequin, dressed it garishly, and early one morning put it on the toilet in Gavin's private lavatory adjoining his office. It gave Gavin a momentary shock, but no one laughed harder as the story was told and retold.

Friends remember jolly times crewing with him. Herbert learned to sail small boats while he was in high school and joined the Newport Harbor Yacht Club in the 1950s. Owning a progression of sailboats, he ultimately bought a sleek Rhodes 33 and raced competitively and exuberantly for more than 20 years. He gave the boat to his son when golf became his pastime in the 1990s, but admits he misses sailing.

Gavin has maintained a close relationship with his alma mater, the University of Southern California, serving as a USC trustee for more than 25 years. In his college days, he was president of his fraternity, Beta Theta Pi, and became a loyal USC fan. Gavin plucked talented scientists from USC over the years, and the Herbert family has shown a close attachment to the school. His father had graduated from USC, and his four children — Cindy, Laurie, Gavin and Pamela — went there. The tradition continues with several fourth-generation grandchildren who may go there as well.

Awaiting a pie in the face, Gavin Herbert was always a good sport at the Allergan annual employee picnic and carnival.

said. "The formulation with 1.4 percent PVA felt good." The 1.4 percent solution of polyvinyl alcohol became a standard vehicle for carrying a variety of medications to the eye. Jack Browning gave it the soothing name Liquifilm, a name still used 40 years later.

Allergan named the blepharitis drug Blephamide and asked ophthalmologists all over the country to test it. "We got glowing reports back," Boghosian says, "Patients who hadn't been cured for 20 years found the first relief they'd had. Over and over again, the doctors were having spectacular results." Blephamide went on the market in 1960, and when Allergan people went to their first ophthalmologists convention in New York, Blephamide had blazed a trail. Everybody knew who Allergan was.

Gavin Herbert Jr. was making a name for himself as well. Eric Nelson, an early consultant and later research and development director for Allergan, described his first conference with the young CEO and three others from Allergan when Nelson was a professor at the University of California at Los Angeles (UCLA): "Here's this kid — as I saw him — who came for a meeting. The young one, Gavin, was president of the company? Well, two minutes later, there was no question about who was in charge. He sat down at the end of the table, and he knew exactly where he wanted the meeting to go. From then on, I never lacked confidence in Gavin. He was going to make this a major company no matter what."

Raising an Entrepreneur

Gavin and his father shared the same entrepreneurial spirit. In fact, his upbringing had everything to do with his chosen career.

Herbert Sr. had learned his trade as a sales representative for Squibb before starting his own pharmacy. He opened additional stores as cash flow allowed and, after he acquired Horton & Converse in the late 1970s, the chain consisted of more than 20 pharmacies. Jill Lindsay, an early Allergan employee, remembers Herbert Sr. as "an impressive man with wavy silver hair, ice-blue eyes and a certain demeanor about him. When he walked into a room, people kind of stood back." He was an affable man. Dick Williams, one of Allergan's early salesmen, says Herbert Sr. "always did the right thing. He dressed like a diplomat. You just knew he was important."

Gavin's mother, Josephine, was a source of strength. "She had a lot of influence on my life, always encouraging me to do better," he says. "She caused me to believe in the 'power of positive thinking.'" Josephine Herbert Gleis is currently 87 and lives in Newport Beach, California. She has eight grandchildren and seventeen great-grandchildren.

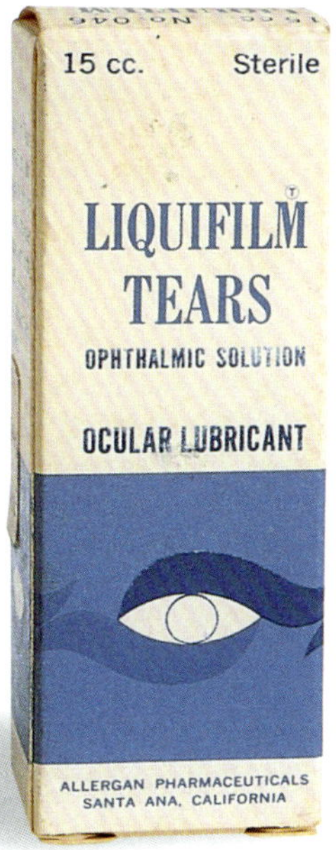

Liquifilm was an Allergan-invented solution that allowed more effective application of both existing and new ocular medications. It became a building block for many Allergan products introduced in the 1960s.

At age 70 she became addicted to a new passion — raising and racing thoroughbred horses. She currently has a stable of more than 20 horses in Kentucky and is very active in this endeavor.

Gavin had his first experience in business at age 13. He and his sister, Marilyn, grew up in a family enjoying what he termed "moderate" income. In 1944, they moved to his grandmother's 10-acre farm in the San Fernando Valley, which included an apricot orchard. World War II was raging, and food was rationed in stores. So young Herbert set up a roadside stand. At the height of the fruit season, he bought a small ad in the *Los Angeles Times*:

"Apricots: You pick 'em. $1 a box."

At 6 a.m. on a Sunday morning the family woke up to blowing auto horns. "I went out, and there were 40 cars lined up," Gavin says. "After sitting under a shady tree letting others do all the picking, I remember walking back at the end of the day with a bundle of small bills — something like $300." Gavin also raised 2,000 or 3,000 chickens to sell as fryers, and sold vegetables grown on the farm. Soon he was an employer; he hired two schoolmates from Van Nuys High to help operate the stand.

Besides making money from the farm, Gavin gained a love for growing things. His grandmother was an amateur horticulturist, "so genetically I probably inherited it," he says. "She'd planted about every plant native to California on her farm." In the 1970s, he indulged his fondness for flowers by investing in Roger's Gardens with his friend Roger McKinnon and later bought McKinnon's share. He and his son, also Gavin Jr., now own it together and have grown it into the largest and most spectacular garden center in

The spirit of invention employed by Allergan scientists, such as Malcolm Boghosian, resulted in products like Liquifilm, which is still marketed today, and Blephamide, which earned Allergan a national reputation for innovative products. Here Boghosian and Allergan employee Rosalie Passany read up on data in the library at Allergan's offices at 1000 South Grand in Santa Ana, California, a facility funded largely by sales of Blephamide. At right, this early price list from 1958 shows the variety of products Allergan was selling as it approached its 10th year in business.

California. Gavin likes the pace of the nursery business: When a new product is developed, it's sold quickly — a pleasant contrast to the years required to bring a new drug to market. "The nursery gave me instant gratification to offset the frustration of the pharmaceutical business," he laughs.

The care of the gardener and the determination of the entrepreneur were equally present in Gavin as he grew Allergan. His aim in running the business, he says, was "to bring the best people together, reward them well and have fun along the way."

"Always hire people smarter than you are," he once advised. But "smarter" is a subjective term. Stuart Eriksen, a scientist who was Allergan's research and development chief for many years, says, "I think Gavin is a remarkable person in his ability to understand science in as much as I don't think he's very scientifically adept. But he was very hard to fool in scientific things. He had a unique ability to know what people would think was worthwhile and whether we'd gone far enough with something. To me that was a major strength. I'd bring up products at a meeting and he'd say, 'That one will sell; that one won't.' And by and large, I think he was right."

"In the early days," Gavin admits, "I was involved in everything — I became a pretty good generalist. One of the hardest things for me in the later years was to really let go and let people do their own thing and not be second guessing. I had to bite my tongue sometimes."

Malcolm Boghosian said Herbert gave him a lot of latitude and "made each person feel like a person who is extremely important. He demanded much of people. I thought it was great." Eriksen adds that in all the years he worked for Allergan "I can truly say that Gavin never asked me to do anything that wasn't right. It's something I can say with a lot of pride as to how the company was run."

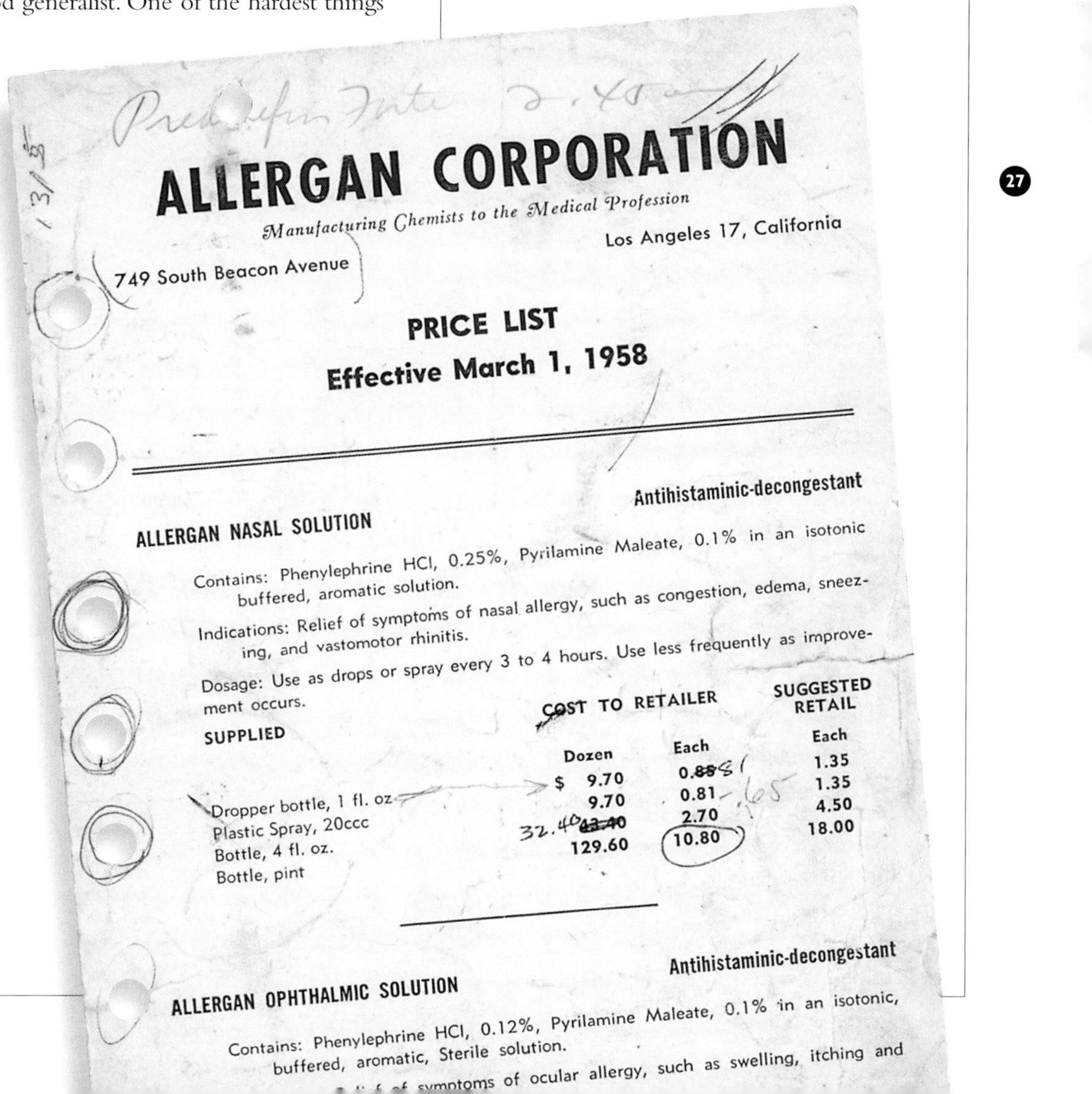

ALLERGAN CORPORATION

Manufacturing Chemists to the Medical Profession

749 South Beacon Avenue — Los Angeles 17, California

PRICE LIST

Effective March 1, 1958

ALLERGAN NASAL SOLUTION — Antihistaminic-decongestant

Contains: Phenylephrine HCl, 0.25%, Pyrilamine Maleate, 0.1% in an isotonic buffered, aromatic solution.

Indications: Relief of symptoms of nasal allergy, such as congestion, edema, sneezing, and vastomotor rhinitis.

Dosage: Use as drops or spray every 3 to 4 hours. Use less frequently as improvement occurs.

SUPPLIED	COST TO RETAILER Dozen	COST TO RETAILER Each	SUGGESTED RETAIL Each
Dropper bottle, 1 fl. oz.	$ 9.70	0.81	1.35
Plastic Spray, 20ccc	9.70	0.81	1.35
Bottle, 4 fl. oz.	32.40	2.70	4.50
Bottle, pint	129.60	10.80	18.00

ALLERGAN OPHTHALMIC SOLUTION — Antihistaminic-decongestant

Contains: Phenylephrine HCl, 0.12%, Pyrilamine Maleate, 0.1% in an isotonic, buffered, aromatic, Sterile solution.

... of symptoms of ocular allergy, such as swelling, itching and

1000

3 Reaching Out

To him whose elastic and vigorous thought keeps pace with the sun, the day is a perpetual morning. — Henry David Thoreau

IN HIS EFFORT TO BUILD THE COMPANY, GAVIN HERBERT JR. BECAME A CONSTANT INTERROGATOR. HE TALKED TO EXPERTS IN EVERY FIELD PERTAINING TO THE BUSINESS, QUERIED CUSTOMERS (BOARD MEMBER HANDEL EVANS ONCE SAID, "I THINK HE KNOWS EVERY OPHTHALMOLOGIST IN THIS COUNTRY") AND QUESTIONED HIS STAFF. DICK WILLIAMS, WHO JOINED THE SALES FORCE IN THE 1960S, SAYS HERBERT "LIKES TO PICK YOUR BRAIN — WHICH IS GOOD BECAUSE YOU THINK, 'I'M REALLY CONTRIBUTING HERE.'"

Santa Ana Chamber of Commerce
CIVIC BEAUTIFICATION COMMITTEE
In recognition of a noteworthy contribution to a more beautiful city, this
1964
GOLDEN 100%
CIVIC AWARD
is presented to
ALLERGAN PHARMACEUTICALS
Greater Pride... Greater Santa Ana

The building at 1000 South Grand in Santa Ana, opposite, was the first built specifically for Allergan. The completed building gave Allergan 30,000 square feet of space for offices, laboratories and production facilities. Its landscaped grounds received an award from the Santa Ana Chamber of Commerce Civic Beautification Committee.

30

The groundbreaking ceremony for the new headquarters building in Santa Ana was a proud moment for those who had laid the foundation for the company. Pictured left to right are Dick Hausman, Fayette Birtcher, an unidentified banker, Keith Herbert (uncle of Gavin Jr. and a building engineer who oversaw construction), Gavin Herbert Sr. and Gavin Herbert Jr. Blephamide, below, introduced to the market in 1960, contibuted greatly to Allergan's bottom line. This and other products introduced throughout the decade would raise Allergan's sales to $10 million over the next 10 years.

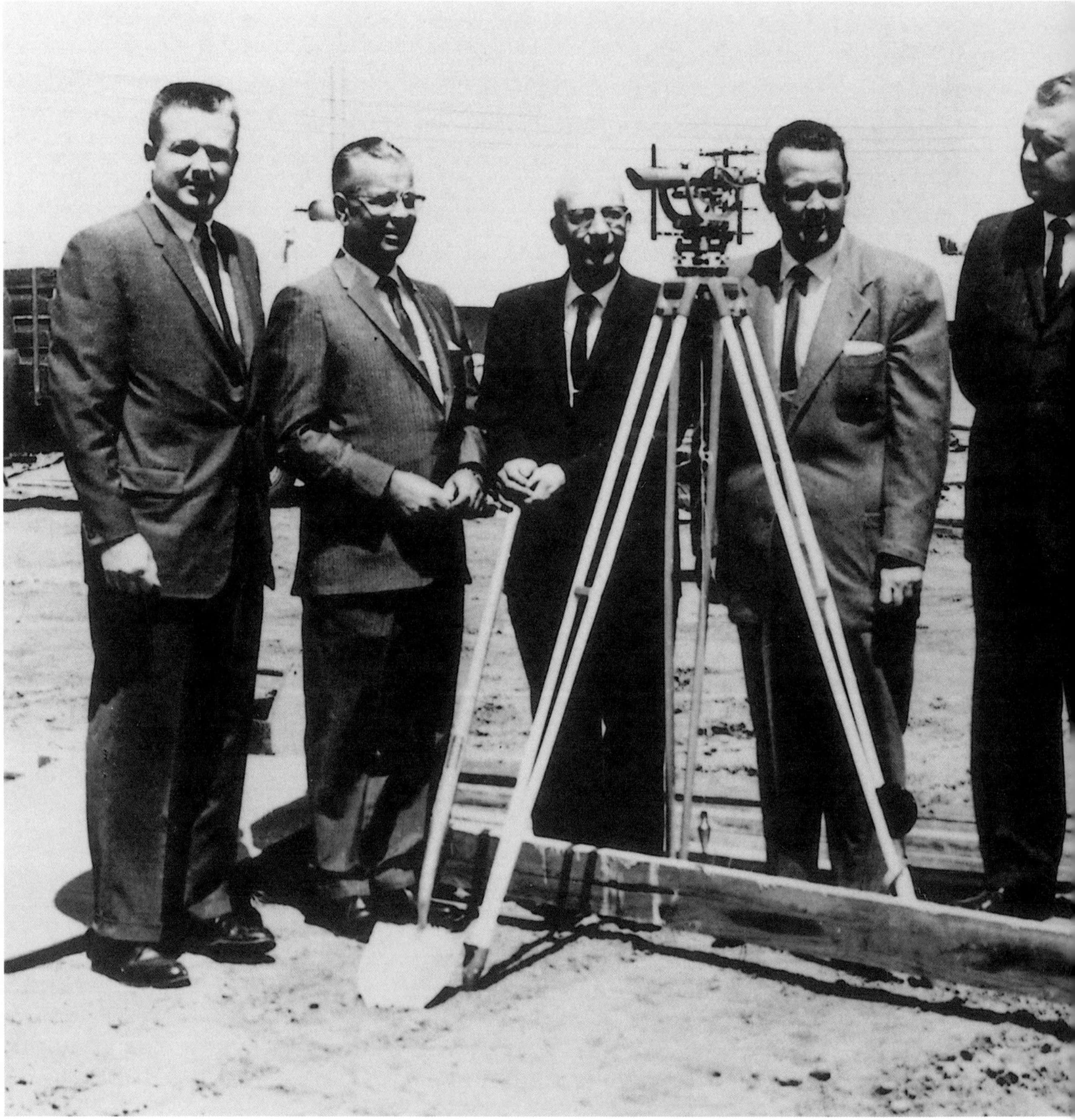

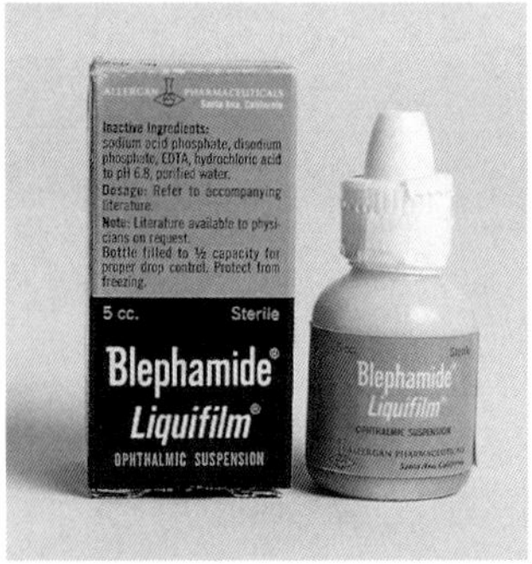

Herbert also seemed to thrive on competition. John Biles, who has known him from the 1950s, agrees: "Oh, he loved it." Biles recalls helping set up an Allergan booth at a national ophthalmology meeting and then checking out the booth of a competitor, Alcon. "Alcon had some data which indicated that its product was the number one product, so that's what was featured in the booth," he says. "Gavin used this to his advantage by grabbing people and saying, 'Come over to Allergan and see what the number two company is doing,' and he made friends."

Part of his ambition for building the company in the face of intense competition was inspired by Jules Stein, founder of the Music Corporation of America and an ophthalmologist, whom Gavin met in the mid-1950s. "He had important, strong thoughts about 'thinking big,' " Gavin says. "I remember him saying there was no difference in time and effort between accomplishing a $1 million project and a $10 million project, and competition declines significantly when you step up an order of magnitude in scale. He always gave me words of advice on thinking big."

Moving Up

With the arrival of the 1960s, Allergan had outgrown its revamped theater and Gavin Herbert was looking for a site to build a larger plant. He chose one in Santa Ana in growing Orange County, California, an attractive area for recruiting new employees.

The 30,000-square-foot Santa Ana structure was ready for occupancy in the fall of 1961. "The cost of the building greatly exceeded our net worth," Gavin says. It was Blephamide, the product that had excited ophthalmologists all over America, that paid for it. Blephamide was among the last formulations that Malcolm Boghosian developed in the old lab in Los Angeles. Allergan introduced it to the market just before moving into the new building, and it soon became the company's largest-selling product. "It was really critical that this product work," Gavin says. "If we hadn't sold the amount of Blephamide we did, we'd have had deep financial problems. When we moved in, we were at about $1 million a year in sales, and I hoped that we might get to $10 million in 10 years — which is about what we did."

This growth was all the more impressive considering the fact that it took place as FDA regulations were becoming more stringent. Not long before the move to Santa Ana, the FDA issued a cease-and-desist order against Allergan's selling of its popular contact-lens-care solution, Liquifilm. The company had filed no New Drug Application (NDA), the Food and Drug Administration charged. Both Herberts (Jr. and Sr.) and Dean M.

From Academe to Allergan

The scientist values research by the size of its contribution to that huge, logically articulated structure of ideas which is already, though not yet half built, the most glorious accomplishment of mankind. —Sir Peter Brian Medawar

Allergan has had close professional ties with university research since the day in 1953 that Gavin Herbert Sr. recruited John Biles, a young USC teacher with a doctorate in chemistry, as a consultant. Through the years, distinguished ophthalmologists, chemists, pharmacologists and other scientists in university laboratories across the country have helped Allergan develop and test new products. Some consultants eventually became full-time members of the company's research and development staff.

Steven Podos, M.D., now chairman of the Department of Ophthalmology at Mount Sinai Medical Center in New York, has been an Allergan consultant from time to time since the early 1970s. Then an assistant professor at Washington University's hospital in St. Louis, Podos had expertise in glaucoma and ocular pharmacology. He conducted the first human studies on Propine and has helped develop a number of drugs for Allergan. He even spent his four-month sabbatical at the company in the late 1980s, consulting with R&D and "learning business techniques from Allergan."

"Most exciting and most helpful to patients," he says, "has been the premium that Allergan has put — and the investment it has made — on research and development of new products. This should be, and often has been, a win-win for the company as well as the patients who benefit from new drugs and discoveries that have been helpful in staving off and/or in curing diseases of the eye."

Podos is executive vice president of an organization called AUPO (Association of University Professors of Ophthalmology). It consists of the chairs of all university ophthalmology departments in the country. Podos has had a further association with Allergan through that group. "In the late 1980s when we were basically an organization that ran out of the pockets of a few chairs, we decided to professionalize," he says, "and Allergan was one of our major donors."

Another of Allergan's long-term academic relationships has been with Morton Goldberg, M.D. A friend of Gavin Herbert's for 30 years, he has been with the Wilmer Ophthalmological Institute of Baltimore, Maryland, as professor and director for the past 10. Soon after accepting the position, he added some 30,000 square feet of research space, and Allergan paid for an entire floor.

"It was space devoted to research and what was then a relatively new field, molecular genetics of eye disease," Goldberg says. "That was only possible because Allergan, through Mr. Herbert's intervention, provided a million-dollar gift. It was then, and I think still is, the leading molecular biology laboratory in eye research. It wouldn't have been possible without Allergan's support." Goldberg says one of Wilmer's lab chiefs has an on-going research relationship with Allergan "studying ligands and other very interesting experimental drugs that may have applicability in treating human eye disease. It has been an enormously successful venture." Goldberg described Allergan as "a highly distinguished company with excellent products that have changed the way doctors take care of their patients in many different disease categories."

Stephen Ryan, M.D., has been associated with Allergan since he became chair of the department of ophthalmology at USC in 1974. He is now senior vice president of medical care and dean of medicine at USC and also is president of the Doheny Eye Institute, Los Angeles.

"I think Allergan has always been at the forefront in developing new products that benefit eye patients and for eye care," he says. "We could always count on Allergan for quality, and could count on Allergan for providing the right type of products — the important products for the important eye diseases. As a consultant to the company, I've been privileged to see how open they've been to new ideas. Allergan seeks out opinions from ophthalmologist leaders from around the country."

Allergan has had ties to a foundation, Research to Prevent Blindness, for 30 years, contributing to the organization that supports research in about 60 departments of ophthalmology around the country. David Weeks, chair of the foundation, said Allergan has "made a major contribution in providing pharmaceuticals for a number of problems of the eye, and their intraocular lenses have been a contribution, too. I think they've occupied a leadership position in research as far as pharmaceutical things are concerned."

John Shell, Malcolm Boghosian and Eric Nelson, left to right, were instrumental in the development of new products in the 1960s. New FDA regulations required drug companies to prove efficacy of their products to gain FDA approval. Nelson, recruited from the UCLA faculty to be Allergan's research director, helped produce the second drug of any kind to win approval under the new regulations: Herplex, below.

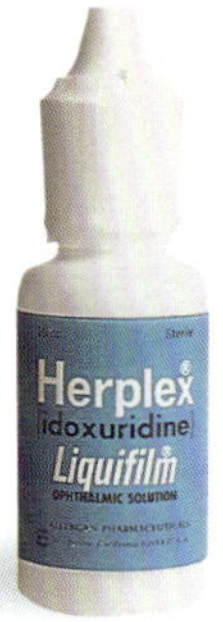

McCann, Allergan's general counsel and an FDA expert, flew to Washington that night. They were able to meet the next day with the FDA commissioner, its medical division head, its general counsel and chief compliance officer. The Allergan team convinced the FDA officials that Liquifilm was properly classified under the law as an "old" drug that didn't require an NDA, and the FDA dismissed the action immediately. The speed of that reversal may be an all-time record. McCann continued as Allergan's general counsel until he retired in 1989.

Soon after Allergan moved, profound changes took place in the Food and Drug Administration. The 1962 "drug amendment acts" passed by Congress removed many products from the market and required, among other restrictions, that to win FDA approval a drug must be shown to be efficacious as well as safe. It was the first time proof of efficacy was required, and it made getting approval far more difficult and expensive than ever before.

Allergan worked quickly to meet the new requirements. The company had established state-of-the-art laboratories in its new plant, and Herbert decided the firm needed a research director. He recruited Eric Nelson, the UCLA professor who had done lab testing for the company at the university, to head it. "He knew I'd been interested in the pharmaceutical industry," Nelson says, "so he offered me a chance to leave the university and come down to Santa Ana to set up the research department, quality control, formulation development, all of that. I'd always been a risk taker, and it sounded like the challenge I'd really been looking for."

Nelson and others from the university established a kind of research that was then new in the pharmaceutical business. "We had a disproportionate number of well-qualified Ph.D.s," Gavin explains. The department focused on new concepts regarding the cellular level of disease and molecular biology. "We were looking at the mechanisms in a cell that were involved in the disease process and then trying to target the causes with some kind of chemical activity," Nelson says. "We were interested in viruses as well as bacteria."

Nelson and his crew believed a chemical closely related to one of the basics of DNA could block the production of the herpes simplex virus, a leading cause of blindness and diminished vision. Out of that research came Herplex, the first anti-viral drug on the market and only the second drug of any kind to win FDA approval under the tough new law.

Herplex sales were modest, but Allergan and the drug got the attention of major pharmaceutical firms and opened the door to in-licensing chemical compounds from them. "We had demonstrated we could operate under the new FDA rules," Gavin says. "This led to the licensing of four or five compounds that fueled our growth in the 1970s. Herplex was a stepping stone."

New Recruits

From the start of his long tenure as CEO, Gavin Herbert had enhanced Allergan's expertise with part-time consultants. As the company prospered, he began recruiting full-time experts for his executive team. Keith C. Lumpkin, who had been with a Los Angeles CPA firm and had worked with Gavin's father on the drugstore chain, came to Allergan to handle finances.

Lumpkin recalls Gavin's recruiting trips east: "He'd come back with a top-flight manager out of a major company. It was incredible. He was just a likeable guy, and he seemed to bring out the best in people who really wanted to perform." Gavin liked to recruit in the winter. "I'd fly them out for a little sunshine," he laughs. "After a time, alarms would go off at two Philadelphia pharmaceutical firms whenever we came to town." Henry Wendt, then a SmithKline & French executive and now a member of Allergan's board, says, "One of his favorite recruiting positions was on the steps of Wills

The Saddleback Inn in Santa Ana was the site of Allergan's first national sales meeting in 1967. With the help of Marv Sargent, Allergan's sales force had been expanded from solo salesman Glenn N. Pughe. These "new recruits" of the 1960s were keys to the future success of the company, and many remained with Allergan for the better part of their careers, becoming 20- and 30-year veterans.

Eye Hospital in Philadelphia, catty-corner across the street from the headquarters of SmithKline & French. He picked off a few SmithKline people in the 1960s."

Dick Hausman, Herbert's brother-in-law and an early company executive, says, "It was exciting at Allergan. I was doing things I hadn't really been trained for, and I couldn't rely on past experiences." Eric Nelson recalls everyone working late and gathering in Gavin's office to review the day's events. As Gene LaPorte, another early executive, explains, "I think the company's destiny was probably decided in his office after five o'clock."

Over the years, Herbert occasionally took his management team to his mountain cabin in Idyllwild, California, for "management off-site" sessions. He usually challenged his team with questions. Richard Ulmer, a former executive, talks about the retreats: "It was wonderful. We'd go for walks, have barbecues in the evening and work our tails off during the day. A question he asked over and over was, 'If you had an extra million dollars to invest, and you had this management team and it was suddenly your decision, what would you do with it to grow the business?' "

Allergan also began building a sales force in the 1960s. Glenn Pughe had joined as the first salesman when it was so small he helped mix formulas in the old lab. In 1960 Herbert recruited Marv Sargent to develop a team of sales representatives nationally while Pughe handled Southern California marketing. Until then, national sales were done solely by mailings to doctors. Sargent hired representatives in New York, Philadelphia, New Orleans, Chicago and San Francisco. Dave Saylor was the second person Sargent recruited onto the sales staff. Saylor, who would later become Allergan's director of trade and professional relations, had worked for Eaton, another pharmaceutical company, but felt he was getting nowhere. "I guess what attracted me to Allergan was the challenge," he said, "a brand new company — lots of competition and vision. I liked that."

Because contact-lens-care products were sold over the counter in drugstores, Saylor and other salesmen needed promotional assistance in this market too. "We had our wives go to a dozen drugstores and ask for Allergan products," he says. "I think my wife found Liquifilm bottles in two, which she bought. All the others promised to put it in." During a long career with Allergan, Saylor wrote what were at the time the company's largest orders: one for $5,000 in the early days, and many years later, one for $3 million.

Promotional mailings would continue to be an important sales method, and Gavin and Sargent hired Dick Williams in 1961 to profile ophthalmologists on Allergan's national mailing list. Williams, who had been working in a Southern California pharmacy and was interested in marketing, suggested rating doctors on volume of business so the salesmen would know where to concentrate

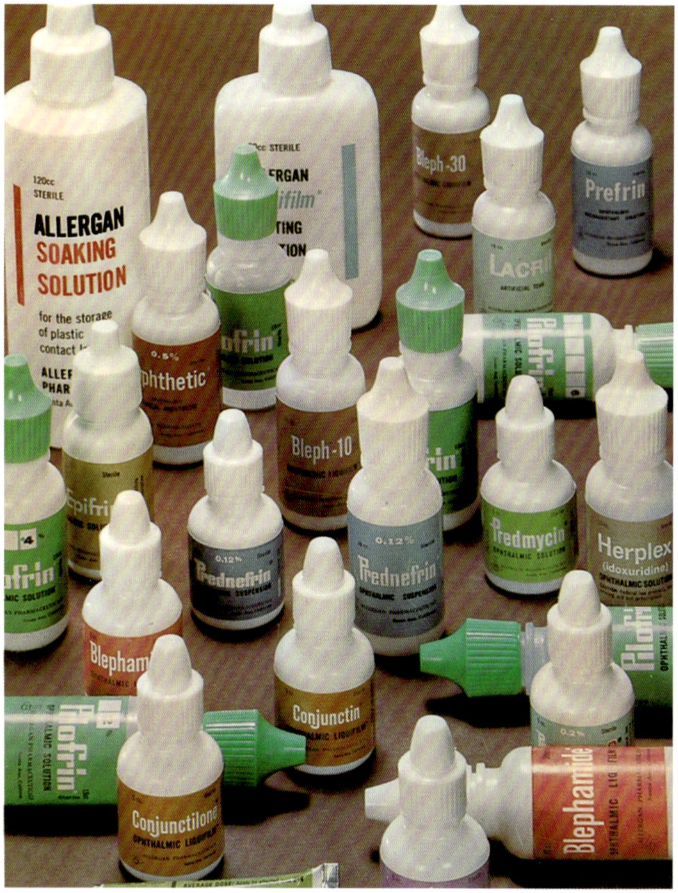

Allergan's 1963 product lineup boasted some early contact-lens-care products. The introduction of these over-the-counter products sent Allergan's sales staff into the offices of optometrists for the first time. It also sent Allergan employees and their wives "undercover" to pharmacies to see if Allergan's salesmen were succeeding in getting the company's over-the-counter products on the shelves.

their efforts. He started on a six-month nationwide tour that included visits to about 2,300 ophthalmology offices, talking to the receptionist, checking the number of patients in the waiting room, getting an idea of how busy the doctor was. From this research, Allergan generated a profile for each doctor, which listed the doctor's practice specialty, the average number of patients per day and the potential to buy pharmaceuticals from Allergan, enabling Allergan to focus its marketing effort.

When that job was finished, Williams became sales rep for all of Northern California and developed several techniques of his own. He catered to ophthalmology residents in the major hospitals, knowing that they were tomorrow's doctors. He also ignored the occasional enmity between medical doctors and optometrists and promoted lens-care products to the optometrists with considerable success.

As the national sales force grew, all the salesmen's cars were equipped with tape decks. The sales manager or medical department would tape a message about a particular product and send copies to the salesmen to listen to as they traveled from one call to another. Sales people were few during the 1960s, and each had many miles to travel calling on ophthalmologists. Bailey Crumpler, who joined the company as a sales rep and later became a district sales manager, says, "You had to put in a lot of time behind the wheel, but the good thing was that doctors were very receptive. It was a pleasure to go to doctors' offices because they wanted to see us. We kept them informed."

The early salesmen recall the unique quality that drew them to Allergan. "It had a real family atmosphere for the first 20 years I was there," says Crumpler. "If you were doing your job, they wanted you to have a home." Dave Saylor says, "In some of the

Ron Ascherman, left, Keith Lumpkin and others gave Allergan a marketing advantage in the early 1960s by using the company's IBM 360-20 computer to store customer profiles and generate cleverly personalized sales letters.

Bea Wittig joined Allergan in 1955 as Bea Alt when Allergan had only six full-time employees. She ran the direct mail department in the 1960s and later the international packaging department, where she instituted systems still in place. Bea retired after more than 30 years with the company.

bigger companies you were a number; here you were a name."

And in the small, growing company, each member of the team felt responsible for building the company's sales. "It was hard work and long hours," Gene LaPorte recalls. "Gavin expected more than you ever thought you could deliver, but it was enjoyable doing it. Every morning I looked forward to going to work. We balanced the busy workdays with impromptu gatherings after work and had a celebration whenever Allergan passed a key milestone: biggest order, strongest sales month, new drug approved."

"Fun was part of our philosophy," Gavin says. "You should enjoy what you're doing." But fun never interfered with growing the business.

Gene LaPorte played catcher on the Allergan Beavers ball club and managed the team. About 6:30 one evening a game was on, and suddenly Gavin Herbert came running onto the field. "I was glad I had the catcher's gear on because I could tell he was angry," LaPorte says. "He said, 'You're playing baseball? We're back-ordered and you're playing baseball?' I said, 'It's in sterility test and there's nothing I can do but wait.'" He let it go, but it was clear that "back-ordered" was the last thing Gavin wanted the company to be.

Some of the push toward production deadlines was eased by developing technology in the plant. In 1961, a major production frustration was sterile filtration. The equipment, called a Seles Candle, "took about a day to do the filtration and about a week to clean the filter," according to Malcolm Boghosian. He and a salesman persuaded Herbert to buy an expensive Millipore filter, which pushed 45 liters of solution through in about two minutes. Herbert was so proud of it, he brought his father in to see it work. "We had it all set up to go," Boghosian said, "and a hose pops off and squirts all over him, the chairman of the board. Great demonstration." The filter, hose reattached, helped prevent the loathed back-ordering.

For all its camaraderie and small-company culture, Allergan was taking better advantage of technology than many of its larger competitors. It was among the earliest companies to use computers extensively. Keith Lumpkin introduced a data-processing system in the business office in 1962. Field representatives compiled customer profiles that were entered in the company computer, an IBM 360-20. The data on doctors made possible personalized (but computer-generated) letters and sample mailings.
A marketing expert at the time remarked that Allergan's progress and plans were among the most sophisticated he'd ever seen. Communication to all Allergan employees improved when Jim Batoosingh, who was handling quality control, started a newsletter, *Eyelites*. It has taken several forms over the years, but an all-employee publication has been part of Allergan ever since.

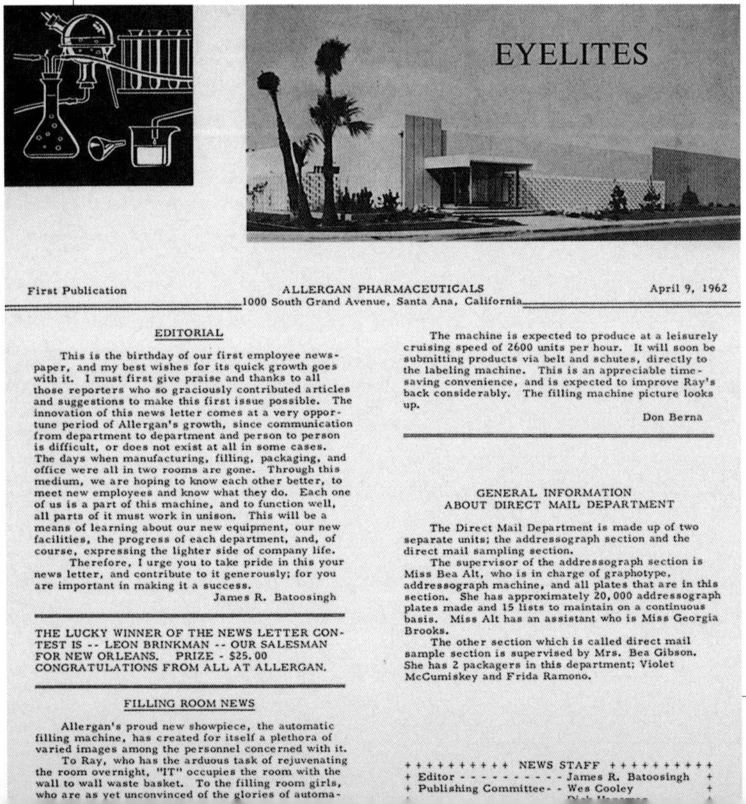

EYELITES

First Publication — ALLERGAN PHARMACEUTICALS — April 9, 1962
1000 South Grand Avenue, Santa Ana, California

EDITORIAL

This is the birthday of our first employee newspaper, and my best wishes for its quick growth goes with it. I must first give praise and thanks to all those reporters who so graciously contributed articles and suggestions to make this first issue possible. The innovation of this news letter comes at a very opportune period of Allergan's growth, since communication from department to department and person to person is difficult, or does not exist at all in some cases. The days when manufacturing, filling, packaging, and office were all in two rooms are gone. Through this medium, we are hoping to know each other better, to meet new employees and know what they do. Each one of us is a part of this machine, and to function well, all parts of it must work in unison. This will be a means of learning about our new equipment, our new facilities, the progress of each department, and, of course, expressing the lighter side of company life.

Therefore, I urge you to take pride in this your news letter, and contribute to it generously; for you are important in making it a success.

James R. Batoosingh

THE LUCKY WINNER OF THE NEWS LETTER CONTEST IS -- LEON BRINKMAN -- OUR SALESMAN FOR NEW ORLEANS. PRIZE - $25.00
CONGRATULATIONS FROM ALL AT ALLERGAN.

FILLING ROOM NEWS

Allergan's proud new showpiece, the automatic filling machine, has created for itself a plethora of varied images among the personnel concerned with it.

To Ray, who has the arduous task of rejuvenating the room overnight, "IT" occupies the room with the wall to wall waste basket. To the filling room girls, who are as yet unconvinced of the glories of automa-

The machine is expected to produce at a leisurely cruising speed of 2600 units per hour. It will soon be submitting products via belt and schutes, directly to the labeling machine. This is an appreciable time-saving convenience, and is expected to improve Ray's back considerably. The filling machine picture looks up.

Don Berna

GENERAL INFORMATION
ABOUT DIRECT MAIL DEPARTMENT

The Direct Mail Department is made up of two separate units; the addressograph section and the direct mail sampling section.

The supervisor of the addressograph section is Miss Bea Alt, who is in charge of graphotype, addressograph machine, and all plates that are in this section. She has approximately 20,000 addressograph plates made and 15 lists to maintain on a continuous basis. Miss Alt has an assistant who is Miss Georgia Brooks.

The other section which is called direct mail sample section is supervised by Mrs. Bea Gibson. She has 2 packagers in this department; Violet McCumiskey and Frida Ramono.

+++++++++++ NEWS STAFF +++++++++++
+ Editor - - - - - - - - - - - James R. Batoosingh +
+ Publishing Committee - - Wes Cooley +

As Allergan grew bigger, it needed a vehicle to communicate to all employees and keep them informed about progress on various fronts. This first issue of *Eyelites* was put out by Jim Batoosingh in April 1962. *Eyelites* was the first of several company newsletters that have proudly served the same purpose and an indication of Allergan's increasingly modern marketing and communications tools. *Eyelites* was the predecessor of today's *Insight* magazine.

A Look Overseas

When Gavin Herbert had an expansion idea, he generally acted on it. "In 1963 Gavin and Dick Hausman were thinking we ought to be doing something overseas," recalls Eric Nelson, Allergan's research chief at the time. Nelson spoke Swedish and German and was planning a trip to visit relatives in Sweden. So they suggested Nelson extend the trip and explore the possibility of partnering arrangements with companies in several European countries. Nelson traveled for 10 weeks and brought back information that would help Allergan establish an international presence.

One of Nelson's initial contacts from that trip was a Swedish firm, LEO. Several years later, two distinguished scientists from that company came to Allergan to discuss research on prostaglandins, powerful hormones or hormone-like substances. Gavin arranged a welcome dinner in their honor at the Newport Harbor Yacht Club in Newport Beach, California.

"We had dinner and then Gavin brought in some Tahitian friends and musicians," Nelson says. "Pretty soon they had these two guys out there doing dances. They had a wonderful time, and it really cemented our relationship." The visitors were equally impressed with Allergan's research savvy, and a 10-year joint research effort resulted.

Meanwhile, a search was under way to find overseas distributors who would promote Allergan products. Allergan hired Bud Schaefer, a young graduate of an international business school, to lead the effort. For a time he, Keith Lumpkin (finance) and Dick Hausman (international division president, among other titles) traveled frequently to foreign distributors to give a personal Allergan touch to the relationships Schaefer had established.

In 1964, the company established Allergan of Canada, Ltd., with headquarters in Montreal to package, label, distribute and promote the company's products in Canada. Four years later Allergan opened a subsidiary in Australia and, in addition, arranged a joint venture with Laboratorios Sanfer/Mexico to manufacture its complete line in Mexico City. Initially, overseas business was a small fraction of Allergan's sales. "But we saw that it could become a major part of the company," Lumpkin recalls. Today international sales account for well over half of Allergan's business.

Canada was one of the earliest and most important markets for Allergan. Until laws changed and products could be imported from the U.S., Canada was also an Allergan manufacturing site. On the left are Keith Lumpkin and Gilles LaBonte (with dark glasses), a popular Allergan of Canada, Ltd., sales manager whose life was cut short by a tragic airplane crash.

Creative Selling

Sales efforts in the United States intensified in the 1960s. Allergan sent a stream of "Dear Doctor" letters to ophthalmologists all over the country, each one promoting a single product. Most were signed by Lewis H. Evans, who sometimes used the title director of professional services and sometimes sales manager. Occasionally, one was signed by Gavin Herbert or by Eric Nelson. It was actually Jack Browning, director of Allergan's promotion, who wrote them all, devising distinctive characteristics for each signer.

A typical Evans letter comprised half a dozen short, chatty paragraphs describing without excessive fluff the advantages of Blephamide, Epifrin, Herplex or Liquifilm, and often enclosing a card the doctor could return if he or she wanted samples. Shorter memos accompanied sample bottles. For one non-prescription product Browning often sent doctors picture postcards of beaches

"Dear Doctor" letters were the key element of Jack Browning's marketing campaign to ophthalmologists. Postcards and personal notes were part of the program to get doctors thinking about Blephamide and other Allergan products.

or ski resorts with a message in longhand such as:

"Whether from wind, sun on the slopes, throwing snowballs or just 'socializing' in the chalet, the red, irritated eye is a common complaint...and Prefrin Liquifilm is the uncommon solution.... Don't you think your 'active' patients would appreciate hearing about it?"

Browning and Jim Haskel, a copywriter working with him, prepared doctors' brochures containing both promotional and technical information and bought page ads in ophthalmology journals. They published an *Ophthalmic Prescription Handbook* that included all ophthalmic products made by any pharmaceutical company. Allergan sent the hard-bound book free to all ophthalmologists, and it was well received.

All the commotion helped bring the young company to the attention of the nation's ophthalmologists. Allergan had two

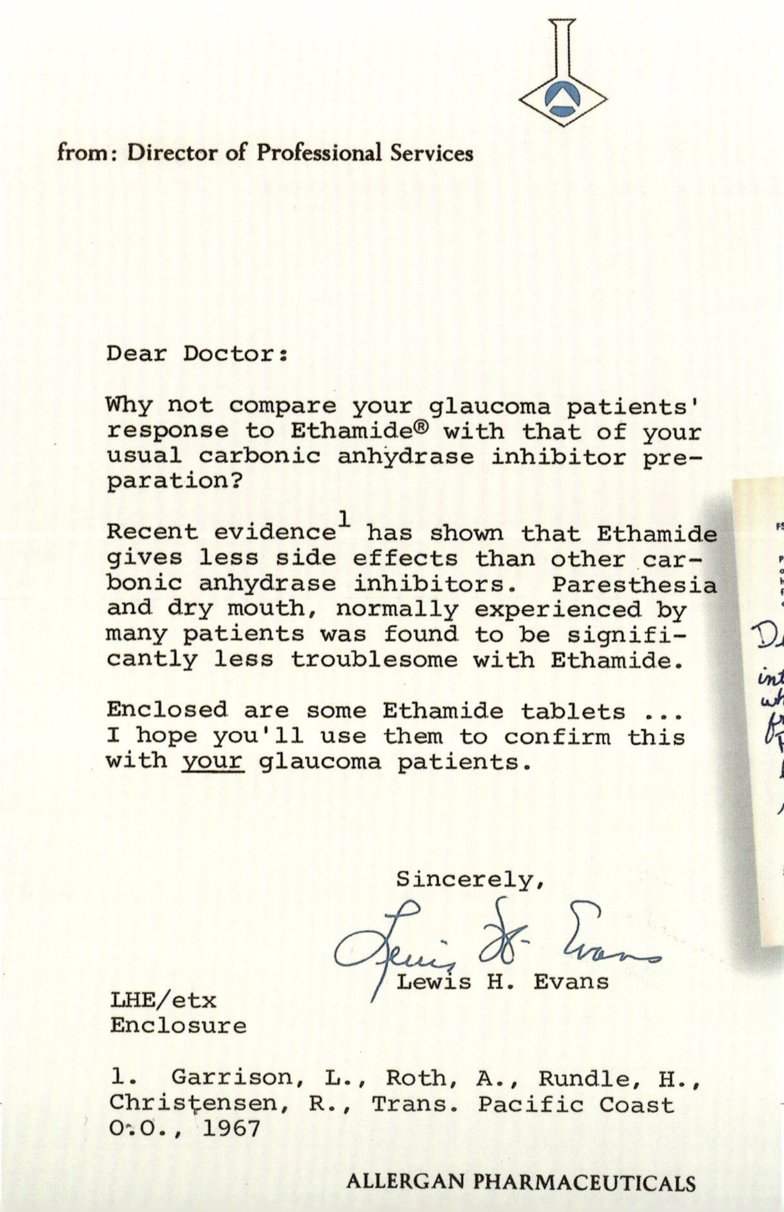

from: Director of Professional Services

Dear Doctor:

Why not compare your glaucoma patients' response to Ethamide® with that of your usual carbonic anhydrase inhibitor preparation?

Recent evidence[1] has shown that Ethamide gives less side effects than other carbonic anhydrase inhibitors. Paresthesia and dry mouth, normally experienced by many patients was found to be significantly less troublesome with Ethamide.

Enclosed are some Ethamide tablets ... I hope you'll use them to confirm this with your glaucoma patients.

Sincerely,

Lewis H. Evans

LHE/etx
Enclosure

1. Garrison, L., Roth, A., Rundle, H., Christensen, R., Trans. Pacific Coast O.O., 1967

ALLERGAN PHARMACEUTICALS

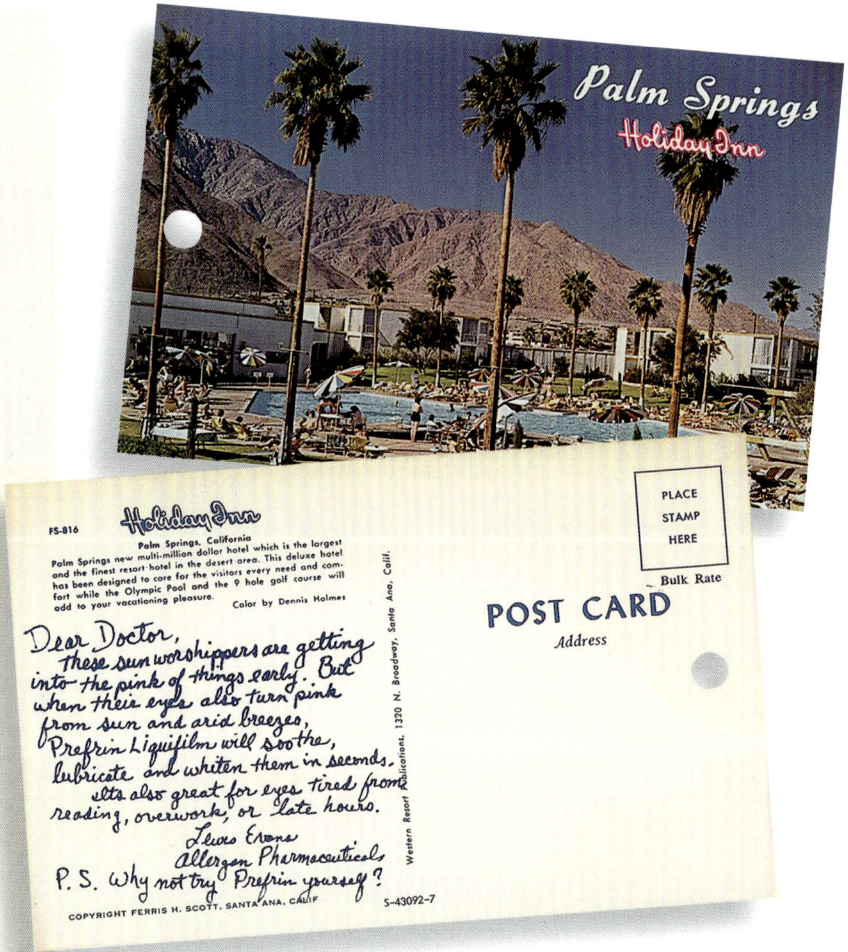

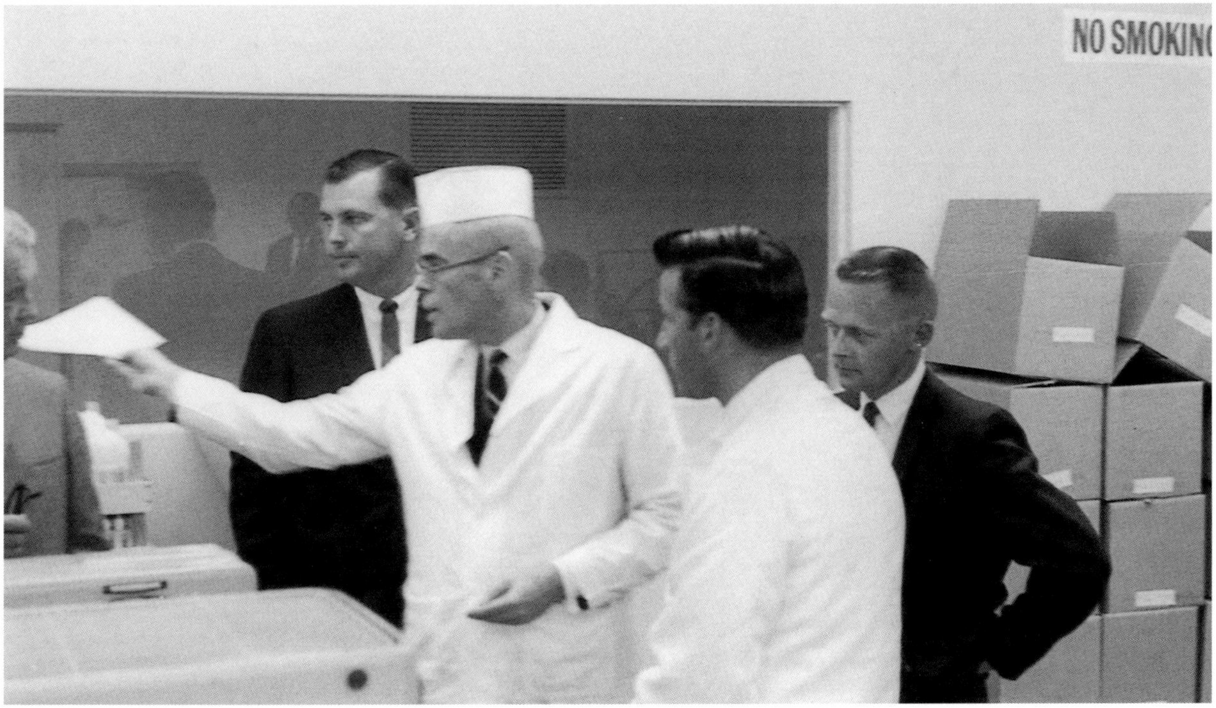

FDA Commissioner James Goddard was invited to visit Allergan's facilities in 1966. It was an unusual request and even more unusual that Goddard accepted. Here Goddard (wearing a hat) talks with, left to right, Gavin Herbert Sr., Gavin Jr., Gene LaPorte and Harry Sponnable. The relationship enabled Allergan to make key contacts and invaluable friends in both the pharmaceutical industry and the government.

displays at the American Academy of Ophthalmology and Otolaryngology in Chicago in 1964, and more than 1,500 doctors stopped by — twice as many as expected.

During ophthalmology conventions, Allergan always had hospitality rooms for the doctors who attended to meet the Allergan management team. "I guess the most memorable for me," Keith Lumpkin says, "was the first one they had at the New York Hilton. I don't know how many people we had there — hundreds — a lot more than we could afford. I was worried about paying the bill." Lumpkin demanded that the hotel give a full accounting of expenses in each room Allergan people used. "It took the hotel about a month to get all this together," he says. "That gave us time to make enough sales to pay for this gala affair."

In the 1960s, Allergan began a series of doctors' seminars, sometimes run during conventions and sometimes by flying a group of doctors to Allergan headquarters. "We decided it would be useful to bring together, for example, the glaucoma experts for two or three days of brainstorming," Eric Nelson said. "We would take notes about what was needed in the field. So we had all this information to work on later and to use as we designed the products. These experts were then very willing to test a resulting product. They wanted to talk about it, publish studies about it, become experts on the new drug. We got the very best people, and it proved to be very successful."

The company restructured its marketing organization in 1964, forming a new division to handle all contact lens products: Liquifilm Wetting Solution, Allergan Soaking Solution, Liquifilm Tears, and Prefrin Liquifilm. In 1965, the company added LC65 Cleaning Solution to the list and began an aggressive sales campaign in drugstores across the country. The effort included designing a compact tray labeled "Contact Lens Care Center" and installing the displays in over 10,000 stores.

Modern Methods and Management

The company expanded its research and development work in 1965 by hiring Stuart Eriksen, an associate professor of pharmacy at the University of Wisconsin. Up to that time FDA approval for new drugs was done largely on the clinical judgment of physicians — no statistics and few controlled, double-blind studies. Allergan management realized that with new FDA chief James

Goddard and new rules, changes were in store. "I came on board to oversee clinical studies and to evaluate the results," Eriksen says. "The studies were run by outside physicians, but I saw to it that the studies were publishable and could be filed with the Food and Drug Administration. The FDA had begun to demand pharmaceutical companies interpret the data with bio-statistics, and I had experience in clinical research."

A key event, in 1966, was when Bill

Allergan's board of directors, pictured here in 1967, was a forward-thinking group of managers and scientists that would eventually take the company public. From left to right are: (back row) Dean M. McCann, Gavin S. Younkin, Hazen Boucher Jr., E. M. Gherman, Thomas E. "Ed" O'Sullivan, John G. "Jack" Monkman and John A. Biles. (front row) Keith C. Lumpkin, Gavin S. Herbert Sr., Gavin S. Herbert Jr., Richard P. Hausman and Eric L. Nelson. (Not shown is Robert Hardt.)

Shepherd came on board. A one-time Navy diver and a UCLA graduate with a degree in biochemistry, Shepherd took a pay cut from his job at Ford Philco to join Allergan as a formulation chemist. "I realized after I'd worked here a couple of years that I liked working with people better than working in the lab, even though I loved chemistry," Shepherd says. "It was more challenging and more rewarding." Eight years after joining Allergan he went back to college part time and earned a master of business administration degree. In a 31-year career with Allergan he would progress through a series of key jobs and a variety of titles — head of development, quality-control chief, head of operations, president of the Allergan corporation — to become chief executive officer and chairman of the board.

Bill Shepherd joined Allergan in 1966 as a bench chemist and would eventually serve as chief executive officer and chairman of the board. He had an inquisitive mind and learned about the company from the bottom up, leaving the lab for management positions that offered him more opportunity to work with people.

In 1969, with its niche in ophthalmology well-established, Allergan decided to enter the field of dermatology as a second specialty. The company would be dealing with a relatively small group of specialists, so the field lent itself to the kind of marketing strategy the company knew well. In addition, most dermatologic drugs were topical, many of them similar to those used in ophthalmology — i.e., topical steroids — which Allergan had expertise formulating.

Believing that a separate image for the dermatology market would appeal to the specialists in that field, Allergan established a division called G. S. Herbert Laboratories to manufacture and market skin-care products. "The new company was an effort to create identity and translate that identity to a face," Gavin explains.

Gavin Herbert Sr. — chairman of the board and still present in the office part-time and at important company events — joined Gavin Jr. and other staff members in the continued practice of visiting doctors and questioning them about their needs. "We'd go to the meetings of dermatologists and get to know them personally," Gavin says. "They liked the idea that we were the principals of the company." G. S. Herbert Laboratories continued as a division for more than 25 years and then was absorbed into Allergan.

Late in the 1960s, as Allergan was approaching annual sales of $10 million, the company had its first $400,000 month. Of course, that called for a celebration. Stuart Eriksen tells about it: "We brought everybody in and served champagne. The Allergan Beavers had a ball game that night, and all the players were in that room. We discovered we were in trouble when we trotted out onto the field and the center fielder tripped over second base and fell flat on his face."

By 1965, Allergan had outgrown the plant that had seemed so big four years earlier. The company leased another Santa Ana building for part of its operations, and about a year later, the Allergan newsletter carried a drawing of a proposed administration building for the Santa Ana site. In the view of board member John Parker, however, the building was too expensive for the neighborhood, and a search began for a larger site. Allergan acquired 24 acres of a 635-acre area in Irvine called University Industrial Park on a lease-purchase plan.

At the time, the whole "park" was empty land. "A lot of people thought we were crazy," Herbert said. "Our sales were only $7 or $8 million." The land cost $32,000 an acre. Today, if there were any bare land left in the upscale industrial park it would be worth more than a million dollars an acre. The first structure built on the property was a 60,000-square-foot production building. The rest of the company operations remained in Santa Ana. Allergan would have to come up with a plan to fund a new headquarters building and research and design center to suit the rapidly growing company.

New Products, New Quarters

Why, then the world's mine oyster... — *The Merry Wives of Windsor,* William Shakespeare

ALLERGAN PHARMACEUTICALS BECAME A PUBLIC COMPANY ON OCTOBER 8, 1970, WHEN IT ANNOUNCED THE ISSUANCE OF 280,000 SHARES AT $15 A SHARE. "I HAD LOOKED FORWARD TO GOING PUBLIC FOR SOME TIME," GAVIN HERBERT SAYS. HE HAD SET UP A BOARD OF DIRECTORS LIKE THAT OF A PUBLIC COMPANY SEVERAL YEARS BEFORE, AND WHEN HE PRESENTED THIS IDEA TO THE BOARD, IT PASSED EASILY. "IT WAS AN EXCITING TIME," HE RECALLS. "IT WAS A VERY VOLATILE TIME IN THE STOCK MARKET, WITH THE HIGHEST PRICE-EARNINGS RATIOS PHARMACEUTICAL STOCKS SAW UNTIL THE LATE 1990S."

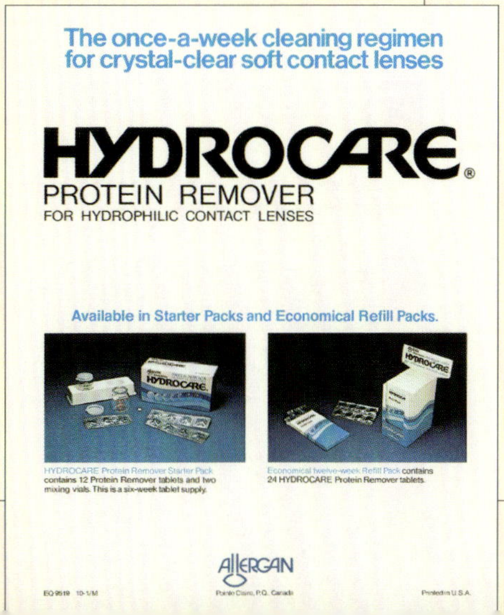

This aerial view of Allergan's worldwide headquarters shows the initial tower that was constructed (right foreground) and the first production building (left foreground). Behind the tower is Allergan's warehouse, with Fluor Corporation's complex rising in the center of the photo. HydroCare, one of Allergan's first contact-lens-care products, was manufactured at this new facility. In the distance one can see the old El Toro marine base and Saddleback Mountain on the horizon.

To prepare for going public, Allergan cut part of its research costs by spinning off a company called Nelson Research and Development, headed by Eric Nelson. Allergan owned part of Nelson Research but the new firm also raised money from investors. The idea was to relieve Allergan of costs for research concepts focusing on receptor site design that could bring nothing to the marketplace for several years. To offset these costs, Nelson Research would license discoveries to other pharmaceutical companies as well as Allergan.

Gavin Herbert Jr. formally receives funds from the public offering of Allergan stock from banker Charlie Bond of United California Bank while Dick Hausman (far left) and Keith Lumpkin (far right) look on in early 1971. The IPO provided the funds to build the complex that still serves as Allergan's worldwide headquarters in Irvine, California.

Nelson Research designed new molecules in basic research, similar to the kind now going on in Allergan's much-expanded research department. It became deeply involved with the University of California at Irvine (UCI) and eventually built its headquarters on the campus. Nelson Research became a public company for several years and was later sold and moved to Virginia. Its campus building was turned over to the medical school at UCI.

Norris Battin, a marketing expert Gavin had recruited from SmithKline two years earlier, joined a team headed by Bob Fosberg introducing Allergan as a promising investment. "We'd go around the country on a road show and present the company to investors, deal with security analysts, handle communications," Battin said. A prospectus announcing the stock offering listed company sales for 1969 at just over $8 million, more than twice the gross of three years earlier. It had 28 products on the market, all in the fields of ophthalmology and dermatology.

Of the money generated by the stock sale, approximately $2 million went back into the company; the rest went to company shareholders. "We used the money to build a new facility for R&D, marketing and administration at University Park, later known as Tower 1," Herbert says. "In retrospect, that was quite a gamble. But we grew into it pretty fast."

Portrait of a Public Company

In the first annual report a few months after Allergan went public, Gavin's opening statement portrayed a company that was young, flexible, ambitious and frisky. The average age of company officers was 41. The old man of the lot was 46. They were having the most exciting time of their lives. "Despite the seriousness of our business, we try hard not to take ourselves too seriously," Gavin wrote. "We want to enjoy working."

He explained Allergan's strategy, decided years before. As a specialty firm, Allergan was blanketing a few select markets while striving to establish "the kind of personal relationships and the kind of reputation that no company selling to several broad markets can possibly match." Most products at that time were prescription drugs, but solutions for the cleaning and care of contact lenses accounted for about a fourth of the business. Dermatological product sales were about five percent.

The report said the company began work on a drug by "learning all we can about a specific disease or need, and we then hypothesize what kinds of chemical struc-

Jesse Yowell, seated, and Wayne Brabander in microbiology were part of Allergan's quality control team. Here they are testing a sample of product for sterility. With Allergan products being distributed to 56 countries all over the world, such measures ensured that customers in Colombia and Australia got the same quality product as Allergan's Southern Californian neighbors.

tures will give us the desired result. We then check out existing chemicals and, hopefully, develop a product to answer that specific need." It's a method Allergan still uses.

Allergan was selling in 56 countries. Most of these were export markets that Allergan accessed through sales agents, but the company had wholly owned subsidiaries in Canada, Australia, Colombia and Mexico to distribute Allergan products. The Mexican subsidiary also did some manufacturing. But Allergan had not cracked the markets of major European and Asian nations. "We've postponed moving into the larger nations until we have the capital to make an impact," Gavin wrote. That opportunity would come within the decade.

The company had about 350 employees in 1970 and already had established profit-sharing and stock-option plans. Stock ownership, options and bonuses motivated employees and made sure they knew their efforts were appreciated. "We knew we were taking part in a great ride," Norris Battin recalls. "People were young and they had a high spirit and great work ethic for the most part. It was a very stimulating environment."

"Simply stated, a company is really the employees that make it up," says Gavin. "Your success is totally determined by the quality of the team you can put together and your ability to motivate them to achieve extraordinary results. I tried everything I could to recruit the best people and reward the people who were successful. Those that didn't meet the standards were very gently asked to work someplace else. We've never had any labor problems."

Allergan has had three layoffs over the years, which Herbert said he found "personally painful." The company hired an out-

placement agency to help terminated employees find new jobs and worked out a formula for severance pay based on time of employment. With good candid dialogue, Gavin created a high trust level among the Allergan team, to the extent that even people who have left the company generally have a warm feeling about it. A group of them, including both layoffs and retirees among its members, formed an informal alumni association — playfully named "Allergone" that meets for lunch twice a year.

"The Pharm"

Tower 1 and an entry structure, both built in 1971, and a companion tower, built 15 years later, form one of the handsomest corporate headquarters in the prosperous Irvine industrial park. Before construction began, Gavin Herbert and Eric Nelson made a research tour to determine the design of the new building. They visited the offices and research facilities of other pharmaceutical firms and compared the work environment

to the company's level of success.

"One company we visited had situated the research facility 50 miles across town from the corporate offices," Gavin says. "When a company driver tried to take us from corporate to research, he got lost — a bad sign." They eventually settled on a "tower" design similar to one of the top-performing pharmaceuticals. "We felt that a multi-storied building would enhance communication between key departments better than a spread-out low-rise design," Gavin Herbert says.

Bill Shepherd, who oversaw much of the design and construction, says, "Work environment has a lot to do with people's attitude and capabilities. If you provide a great environment they'll probably do better than otherwise." Unlike the glass boxes studding the area, Allergan's headquarters has a sculptured look. Planes and angles of earth-tone brick alternate with tall columns of windows. Three flagpoles front the main building. They usually carry the American, California and Allergan

Amenities like tennis courts and a park-like setting showed Allergan's commitment to a work environment that inspired fresh ideas, clear communication and loyalty. Serious research was undertaken before construction even began to determine campus and building designs that fostered this atmosphere. The result was a facility so picturesque that employees nicknamed it "The Pharm." The first tower of the new headquarters, pictured opposite in 1972, was designed so that with future growth, three towers would eventually surround a common entry. Posing with a model showing the future plans are, left to right, Bill Shepherd, Gavin Herbert, James Cavanaugh, Peter Upton and J. Roberts "Bob" Fosberg.

flags, but when a foreign representative is a guest of the company, he or she finds the flag of his or her nation flying.

The grounds are so park-like that, until the area was fenced, local families sometimes spread their picnic lunches on the grass. Blossoming vines cover a fence near the entry walkway, and a huge array of impatiens beside the walk brightens the entrance. Trees and expanses of lawn abound. Even a parking structure at the back of the grounds has hanging gardens cascading down the wall.

Paintings of old California adorn the inside. Shepherd did most of the selecting. "I'm not sure I'm a good judge of quality, so we hired an outside consultant," Shepherd says. "He brought what he thought was good quality art and then I chose. We bought a lot of California impressionist art before the prices skyrocketed."

When Allergan first moved to the site that employees had dubbed "The Pharm," it included an actual farm for a time. Staff members could plant and tend their own vegetable gardens on the bare land. ("The rabbits had a ball," one employee recalls.) Old timers remember that when the company was smaller and more closely knit, Herbert or Shepherd might suddenly announce that an Allergan milestone had been reached, and there'd be a catered picnic on the lawn. Sometimes the picnic wasn't announced much earlier to the caterer, causing a kitchen crisis a few miles away.

Over the years, Allergan has added other structures. The latest is a $42 million research and development building named for Bill Shepherd. It was built in 1993 and included the input of many Allergan employees. Teams in various research fields designed their own laboratories and even voted on the interior color scheme and art pieces. The result is a pleasant, bright sky-lighted three-story building enhanced with artwork, comfortable sitting areas, snack niches and floor space equal to about three football fields.

The buildings and grounds include a library open electronically 24 hours a day to Allergan people around the world, a fitness center, cafeteria, company store, basketball court, tennis court and a track around a grassy area that serves as a soccer, baseball and Frisbee-tossing field. Another employee benefit is an outside ombudsman, available toll free, to receive any kind of complaint from an Allergan worker.

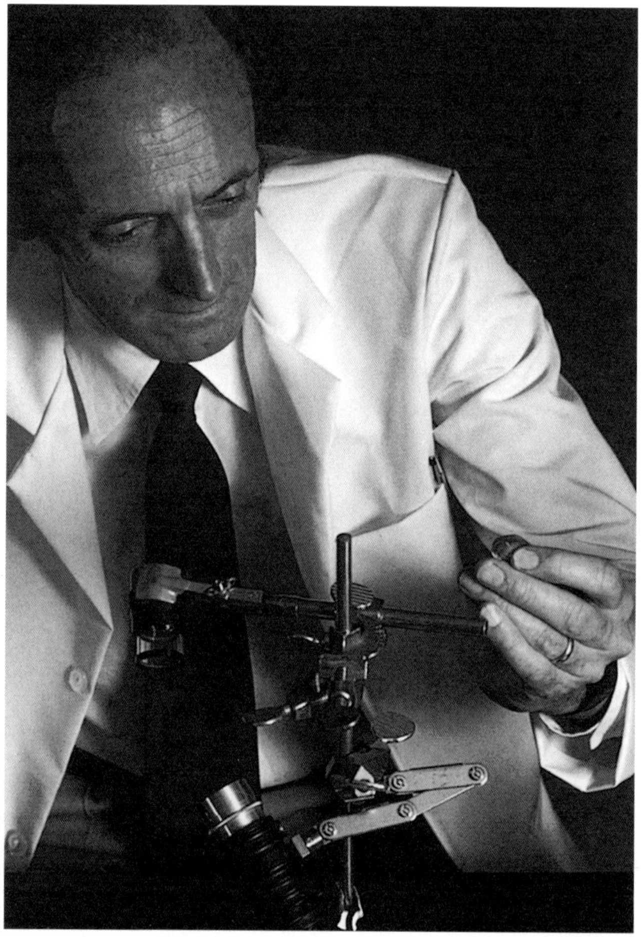

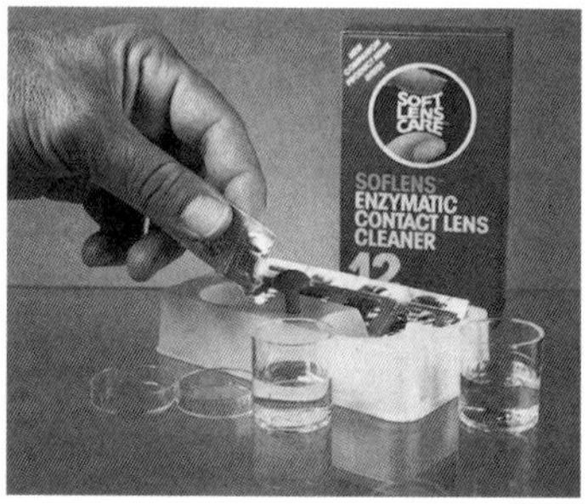

Stuart Eriksen came to Allergan from the University of Wisconsin in 1965 and was instrumental in determining that a stubborn film damaging soft contact lenses was a protein that could be easily removed. Soflens Enzymatic Contact Lens Cleaner was the resulting product that fueled new growth for the company and rescued the soft contact lens market. It was Allergan's first $100 million product.

Leading the Revolution

When Bausch & Lomb introduced soft contact lenses in about 1970, the care of contact lenses was revolutionized. The material of the soft lenses made them more comfortable than hard lenses, but they tended to cloud over with a stubborn deposit after a few weeks. The company contracted with Allergan to develop solutions for cleaning and care. The result was Allergan's first $100 million product, Soflens enzymatic cleaner.

"The whole world said the deposits were fat," says Stuart Eriksen, who headed research and development. "But the research group at Allergan said, 'No they're not; they're protein.'" Two young Allergan scientists, Hampar L. Karageozian and Paul Rudko, discovered that an enzyme in papaya juice removed the protein and was safe for the eyes. They created a product in tablet form. "I think it rescued the soft-lens market," says Eriksen.

The enzyme cleaner became the world's leading contact-lens product, used by close to 10 million people. Its success stimulated copies from other firms, and Allergan's chief patent counsel, Martin Voet, successfully sued both Alcon and Bausch & Lomb — which went from partner to competitor in 1978 — for patent infringement. Ultimately Allergan agreed to license the product to both companies, and they paid substantial royalties for the privilege of using Allergan's patent.

Allergan developed other products for the special care of soft lenses, but not without difficulty. One need was a product to sterilize the lens. "The soft-lens material was very much like a sponge; it soaked up things and held on to them," Gavin explains. "It was tough to find a compound that would kill bacteria without damaging eye tissues. And we needed to find one that didn't bond with or negatively impact the lens material." Another pair of Allergan scientists, Mila Blanco and David Maurer, developed HydroCare soft contact lens disinfecting solution, which met all the requirements and did well in the market.

The soft-lens-care business wasn't the only one that was going strong for Allergan; other new products were fueling Allergan's booming growth in the 1970s. FML Liquifilm won FDA approval as a steroid for treating moderate to severe eye inflammation. Most previous steroids tended to increase intraocular pressure, which could lead to glaucoma. Allergan proved with clinical tests that FML reduced this unwanted side effect. The company also developed a clever hard-lens cleaner, Blink-N-Clean, to clean and re-wet lenses while they're still in the eye.

Bigger Steps Overseas

As sales and breadth of Allergan products increased, the company began looking for more efficient ways to produce and market them. At the beginning of the decade, Allergan established a manufacturing plant in Puerto Rico. To reduce unemployment there, the U.S. government had declared a tax holiday on products made in Puerto Rico and exported to the States. Gene LaPorte, then in charge of production, wrote a report on the possibilities there. LaPorte remembers Gavin told him about a week later, "I've enrolled you in Berlitz; you're going to Puerto Rico." Dick Hausman, executive vice president, flew to Puerto Rico and picked out a site in Mayaguez for the new subsidiary, Allergan America. LaPorte moved to Puerto Rico in February of 1971 to oversee construction, and the plant was in production the following July.

It took some doing. Bill Shepherd remembers watching LaPorte deal with the frustrations of a Caribbean-style approach to work. "The contractor was not putting people on the job," he says. "One night Gene phoned the contractor and said, 'I want to tell you something: I belong to a very big family, and my family is very interested in getting this job done. So I would suggest to you that you have a full crew there tomorrow.' There was a full crew there the next day, and every day after that."

The first shipment of LC65 Cleaning Solution was due from Allergan America on July 1, but the building was still under construction. "We built a room in what was to be my office out of 2-by-4s and clear plastic vinyl," LaPorte says. "We had a laminar flow bench for the air flow that would create the environment we needed. We ran a cord from the plant next door for power, and I borrowed the air compressor from the

In 1971, Gavin Herbert sent Gene LaPorte to Puerto Rico to set up a new manufacturing facility as a subsidiary called Allergan America. The plant was completed in 1972, though not before the first shipment went out from the plant July 1, produced with borrowed equipment. Puerto Rico offered cost-efficient production and savings from government-mandated tax incentives.

Richard Nixon and La Casa Pacifica

Gavin Herbert Jr. is a lifelong Republican who has been active in politics for years. He was co-finance chairman in Orange County for Richard Nixon's second presidential campaign. When La Casa Pacifica in San Clemente became the Nixons' home and the western White House in 1969, Gavin volunteered to maintain the home's extensive gardens. Every time the President journeyed to San Clemente, Gavin mobilized a crew to make sure the house and gardens looked their best. Herbert and Nixon, and their families, became close friends. When Nixon went to China on the 10th anniversary of the Shanghai Communique, he took three friends along with his official entourage — Gavin was one of them.

In the days after Watergate and Nixon's resignation, the men became even closer, taking long walks and sharing personal experiences. It was Gavin who greeted Nixon at the door on August 9, 1974, the day he resigned and flew home to San Clemente. When the Nixons decided to return to the New York City area to be closer to their daughters, La Casa Pacifica was prepared for sale. "As head gardener, I had some privileges — one of them was the right of first refusal," Herbert says. He bought the house in 1980, and its grounds, as one might expect, are among the most beautifully landscaped anywhere. Gavin and his wife, Ninetta, still live in La Casa Pacifica and often entertain family, friends, business associates and Allergan employees in the historic home.

In 1978, Allergan's international team listened as President Nixon delivered a two-hour strategic overview of the global geo-political situation at La Casa Pacifica in San Clemente when it was his home. The group gathered for this photo just outside Nixon's office in the complex.

Irving Leopold was widely regarded as the top ophthalmic pharmacology specialist in the world. He was head of ophthalmology at New York's Mount Sinai Medical Center before joining Allergan's staff on sabbatical. The Allergan culture appealed to him and he became convinced that Allergan provided him a better opportunity for reducing blindness around the world than he would have had in a teaching environment.

painting contractor. On the day we said we were going to run, we ran the products, and they were sterile."

Even after the tax incentive in Puerto Rico was significantly reduced, Allergan continued to operate there, becoming a leading producer of intraocular lenses and surgical products. Allergan will soon phase out pharmaceutical manufacturing there, moving it to Waco, Texas, once capacity at that plant can be expanded.

At the same time the plant was opening in Puerto Rico, Allergan launched its first marketing effort in Europe. Diethart Reichardt was the man who led the charge. Gavin Herbert describes Reichardt as "one of Allergan's heroes, an entrepreneur who made a difference. We gave him a sales kit and a car, pointed him in a direction, and he built a $40 million business."

Reichardt had been working for a small pharmaceutical company in Germany but liked the fact that Allergan focused on eye care, a specialty niche. "That made us a big fish in a small pond," he says. "I jumped in my car and saw everybody I thought was an opinion leader or a potential for business. I was touring for four weeks all over Germany. Then I sat down and developed a market plan. Business was slow at first, but the big breakthrough came in 1974 when we got the enzymatic tablet and later the HydroCare solution. In two years, Allergan became the market leader in Germany."

A German subsidiary named Pharm-Allergan was formed, and it became an American success story in Europe. Reichardt socialized with doctors and took part in ophthalmology conventions. When Irving H. Leopold, a renowned ophthalmologist, became chairman of the Allergan Scientific Advisory Board and a company director, he went to a German convention to lecture at a meeting of glaucoma experts. In 1980, he introduced them to Propine, a new Allergan product to treat glaucoma. Reichardt wrote letters to ophthalmic journal editors inviting them to that and similar meetings. Favorable articles resulted and furthered Allergan's acceptance in Europe.

As business grew, Reichardt hired staff, choosing and training young people because they brought youthful energy to the company. In 1976, Allergan expanded sales beyond Germany to Austria, then Switzerland, the Benelux countries, Italy, the United Kingdom and France.

Gavin took an active role in the development of the European markets, quizzing Reichardt during visits to Europe. As they drove around a country, he would ask about its population, the gross national product, ophthalmic markets, other pharmaceutical markets, Allergan's performance and sales forecasts. "I got a reputation as a terrible driver," Reichardt says, "because as I was driving, he was asking questions and taking notes. That's when you miss a road and find yourself heading in the wrong direction."

Innovations: Successful and Failed

One of the marks of a successful company is constant innovation. Allergan was forever looking for new ways of selling, new areas of business and new partnerships — and some ventures simply didn't work out.

During the late 1960s, Allergan had entered the diagnostic market with new, automated chemical testing equipment that dramatically increased the accuracy of diagnostic tests. Gavin explains, "We were intrigued by the opportunity because of

FDA Commissioner James L. Goddard's finding that 20 to 30 percent of clinical lab tests were inaccurate." Allergan formed a joint venture with G. D. Searle, called Medical Data Center, and began testing the concepts by creating a model clinical laboratory in a visible location on Wilshire Boulevard in Los Angeles.

"We soon found out, however," Gavin continues, "that our efforts to introduce new, high-quality testing methods at significantly lower prices were not appreciated by a number of important physicians who also were customers of Searle. An editorial in the *Los Angeles County Medical Bulletin* complained about drug companies entering the clinical lab business. A week after the article was published, Chairman Jack Searle said he didn't want to offend his customers, so he pulled out of the venture." Allergan continued the project alone until 1969 under the direction of Norris Battin, but "it became apparent that we didn't have the wherewithal to go on, and we discontinued the venture," Gavin says. "What we test-marketed then is standard practice today in the clinical lab business."

One positive outcome was a continued relationship with the Searle family. Three members of the family — Bill and Dan Searle and Wes Dixon — became Allergan investors before the company went public. And Searle later joined Allergan in a joint venture in the United Kingdom.

In another doomed effort to diversify in 1973, Allergan bought 70 percent of California Radiochemicals of Palo Alto, California. Allergan renamed the Palo Alto firm IMAJ International and embarked briefly on a new specialty, nuclear medicine. The idea was sound: IMAJ would make an automated system with which hospital labs could produce Technetium-99, the most widely used radiopharmaceutical. Allergan got product approval and with FDA blessing put machines in several of the most important hospitals in the country.

"Three or four of these things malfunctioned," Gavin recalls. "They leaked radioisotopes in these labs. They had to close for several days and clean things up. It was one of our failures." The 1974 annual report said the company had decided to "concentrate corporate resources on our basic business (ophthalmology and dermatology products) and de-emphasize diversification for the near term." The nuclear-medicine effort cost the company $1.6 million.

But Allergan's innovation was paying off in other areas, and in 1975, the Allergan board declared the company's first dividend on its stock — a nickel a share. Sales were up 30 percent from the year before, and the robust growth continued.

Under the direction of Irving Leopold, Allergan's professional communications took a turn in the academic direction in the 1970s. The company introduced a program called Office Seminars in Ophthalmology. It offered doctors a series of clinical reviews, monographs, audio-visual aids and other materials to keep them abreast of continuing developments in ocular pharmacology and therapeutics. The program continued successfully for several years. Leopold was chairman of an Allergan-sponsored National Symposium on Ocular Pharmacology, held annually for several years.

The year 1977 started on a sad note for Allergan. Gavin Herbert Sr., the first and only chairman of the board, died on January 12. He had lived to see the company he once would have sold for $50,000 become a $50 million firm under his son's leadership. He was enormously proud of the achievement and always enjoyed company events and traveling to Allergan plants in various parts of the world.

Unfortunately, the company's founder did not live to see one of its biggest moments to date. By 1977, Allergan's worth had grown enough to qualify for listing on the New York Stock Exchange. Gavin Herbert Jr. and several of his executives were on the floor of the exchange the first day the Big Board listed Allergan's symbol: AGN. By the end of the decade, strong products and a sophisticated, aggressive marketing strategy devised by two pharmaceutical marketing experts, Norris Battin and Rich Ulmer, vice president of marketing, would turn "most successful year to date" into an annual-report cliche. Tom Bender directed sales and marketing efforts promoting the soft contact lens care products during those years, placing the company in either #1 or #2 position during most of the 1970s and 1980s.

Irish Eyes Are Smiling

By the second half of its third decade in business, Allergan was developing a brisk European business in eye-care products. Shipping them from North America was expensive, and European countries charged duty on imported products, adding to the cost. The European Economic Community (EEC) was coming together. Allergan determined it was time to manufacture within that community and began looking for a site.

Ireland, being a member of the EEC, offered strong incentives to a company that would manufacture goods for export. For years, its own principal export had been its people, often the brightest of them, who sought richer opportunities than Ireland could offer. To stimulate economic development and to create jobs for its citizenry, the Irish government developed a wide array of incentives, including a waiver of all corporation tax, funding for employee training, partnering on construction costs and even building what they called "advance factories" — shells that could quickly house manufacturing operations while plants were being built. Banks offered lease-back arrangements on equipment with low interest — the bank would pay the company to own the assets because the bank could write them off. Two Allergan executives, Bill Shepherd and Ron Taylor, presented these facts to the Allergan board and won approval to find a site in Ireland.

When Allergan's stock listed on the New York Stock Exchange in 1977, Allergan executives Gavin Herbert, Bill Shepherd, Dick Hausman, John Biles, Brian Little and Bob Fosberg, left to right, above, went to New York to watch AGN come up on the Big Board. Proud "father" Gavin Herbert even lit a cigar with Hazen Boucher looking on.

Taylor and Martin Voet, Allergan's associate general counsel, toured Ireland for a month, "looking," Voet says, "at every green field we could find" with a representative of the Irish Industrial Development Authority (IDA). "They're very businesslike and very, very easy to deal with," says Shepherd. "The IDA makes decisions on the spot; there are good business people on the staff." Gavin Herbert and Shepherd joined the search party, finally narrowing it to Portlaoise, about 50 miles from Dublin, and Westport, an attractive seaside town but with the disadvantage of being far from Ireland's commercial center. (When he was asked what the nearest big city was, Ron Taylor would quip, "New York.") Portlaoise seemed to have the edge until someone remarked, "Portlaoise is a fine town, but it's a pity about the high-security prison." Westport got the nod.

But the Allergan board started to second-guess the choice. "You want to do what? Where?" Shepherd mimics. "Westport is 150 miles west of Dublin, a town of about 3,000 people. The board doubted the wisdom of settling there so much that even Gavin got nervous and wondered if we were doing the right thing." The advocates finally persuaded the board, and Voet drew up a contract with the IDA. The Irish government paid about

This aerial view of the idyllic setting of the new manufacturing site in Ireland, centers on the village of Westport. Croaghpatrick Mountain (in the background), where St. Patrick climbed, is a shrine today that brings pilgrims from around the world to follow his footsteps up to the peak. The opening of Allergan's Westport facility draws Catholic and Protestant clergy together to celebrate.

half the cost of the original plant.

Growth was anticipated from the beginning. Allergan immediately acquired options on about 20 acres of surrounding land. The company also acquired a cottage in Westport, rebuilt it to California standards in terms of kitchen and heating, and moved Ron Taylor and his wife in to get Allergan Ireland Ltd. under way.

"I liked Westport," Ron Taylor says. "It was on a seacoast, so it had that little bit of flair as a vacation place instead of being just another old, small town in the midlands." Before actually moving there, Taylor made close to 15 trips in 11 months. "I ran into the same flight attendants so often they thought I worked for the airline," he says. While the first building was being prepared, he set up an office in downtown Westport behind a clothing shop in a 200-year-old building. He had no phone; the little company serving the town had no available lines.

"I'd save up my phone calls," Taylor says, "and once a week, I'd go to the bank for bags of five-pence coins and head over to the post office, which had the only pay phone in town. I'd be on that phone all day long." When he finally did get a phone, it went through a manual exchange, and anybody on the line could listen in. Taylor said sometimes after hours the local operator ("who knew everything about everybody")

would route a call from Allergan headquarters to him at Stephen Walsh's Pub.

Taylor recruited locals to staff the new plant, including the managers. The workers were trained on site; the managers were brought to California "to get an Allergan orientation," he says. One of the early hires was Jim Kiely, who was the general manager. Colam O'Neill, who is now vice president and managing director of Allergan Ireland, came on early as well. "My title at the time was production manager," O'Neill says. "My chores were everything from sweeping the floor and making the coffee to making sure everything was organized for the start up." Before hiring the first hourly worker, Ron

Taylor and other administrators negotiated a contract with the Irish Transportation and General Workers Union to represent all employees in the plant. "They were very good to work with," Taylor says, and they are the only union in any Allergan plant.

The first product manufactured in Ireland was HydroCare, a contact-lens cleaning solution. Half a dozen men — administrators — turned it out on Good Friday of

Allergan made a conscious effort to create a facility that would beautify and benefit the town without disturbing its unique atmosphere. This meant exquisite landscaping with stone walls built the old-fashioned way (without mortar) and award-winning flower gardens throughout the property.

1978. "It took us 20 hours to fill the batch of 7,000 or 8,000 units," O'Neill recalls. "We didn't finish until 6 or 7 o'clock Saturday morning. That was a big landmark in our history. We didn't go straight home, I can tell you. After working all night, we went and had a few pints."

The plant was not only operating but had erected scaffolding for an expansion when Ray Burke, Irish government minister, cut a tape to open it officially. Burke commented that it was the first time in his career that a major expansion was under way on the occasion of a company's official opening. In a booklet commemorating the 20th anniversary of the plant's opening, Shirley Conroy described the early days of Allergan's Westport venture: "High technology? Oh boy, we had typewriters, a few desks, notebooks and manual phones. Yes, we actually had to book all foreign calls through the telephone exchange, and they would ring back when they had a line. Planning? A flip chart with two colors of markers. Canteen? A small coffee dock where we would meet to exchange ideas. Production? Two filling lines with a manual packing operation."

Gavin Herbert took a strong interest in the Irish plant, and he put his usual landscaping imprint on it. "We managed to find some workers skilled in building rock walls without mortar," he says. "We surrounded the property with an old-fashioned rock wall. It really made the people in the town happy. It set it off. It's the sort of thing you can do to help create a sense of pride among employees." Ireland-West Tourism and later Bord Failte (Gaelic for "Irish Tourist Board") awarded Allergan first prize in Ireland for best gardens and external appearance of industrial premises.

By the end of its first year, Allergan Ireland had about 40 employees. "As the markets grew and as the number of products we made were transitioned from the United States and Canada to Westport, the numbers increased," Colam O'Neill says. "We've had nothing but continuous growth." He said it was difficult at first to convince company people in the States that Europe had high-quality sources of supplies. "Everything had to be an exact replica of what was done on the mother ship down to the last piece of string on the parcel," he says. "It took quite a while for people to get comfortable with the fact that outside the United States there was a level of competence and ability to do the same things that were being done in America."

Today the Westport subsidiary employs about 1,000 workers, manufactures all Allergan products except those for skin care and surgery, makes the bottles, labels them and ships products to about 75 countries with labels in each country's language. Enormous technological changes have taken place along with the rapid growth. One is Unitdose technology: The same machine makes the plastic container, then fills it with a sterile product. Automatic testing equipment has replaced test-tube laboratory techniques. Communications employ all the magic of modern electronics. Gamma radiation sterilizes the plastic bottles, a set-up that caused a short-lived political storm in Westport.

"Many years ago we convinced a Dutch company, Gammaster B.V., that it should locate in Westport with a cobalt 60 gamma radiation plant," O'Neill says. "Instead of having to send our bottles outside for sterilization, it's right on our doorstep." But out-of-town agitators spread fears that Westport was importing a monster. The national planning authority called a two-day public hearing. Experts answered every question to the satisfaction of all except the professional objectors. The radiation plant won approval, and apprehension faded away.

Ron Taylor returned to the home office after getting Allergan Ireland off to a sound start, leaving Kiely in charge, and the plant has been operated by Irish nationals ever since. Employees have health benefits, sick pay, end-of-the-year bonuses and a variety of activities promoted by the company. "We have a very active social club," O'Neill says, mentioning the company's 1999 championship football team, "and we support many activities in the community. We've been able to merge into the community without trying to dominate it."

Allergan's presence not only has brought in restaurants, shops and hotels but has stimulated other companies to settle in the area. An entrepreneurial spirit is apparent in the little city. In recent years, Westport has spruced up with smart storefronts and with hanging flower baskets adorning the streets. It has become a popular tourist destination. "It's been exciting to watch our impact on the community," Gavin Herbert says. "We add many millions of dollars to the local economy through salaries, construction, printers and satellite businesses. It has changed Westport in a really nice way. Most of the people employed are those who had moved away because of lack of opportunity and have come back from different places around the world because they wanted to live in their home town."

Alas, there's a down side to every success. An overwhelmingly strong seller's market in housing has resulted. One report said: "As of January 1998, it was not possible for new couples to buy a house in Westport." And Colam O'Neill says, "At the height of the tourist season there's sometimes near gridlock on the town's streets. But Westport has been good for Allergan, and Allergan has been good for Westport."

SOFT LENS CARE
LENS
PLUS

5 Merger with SmithKline

They know enough who know how to learn. — Henry Brooks Adams

IN THE LATE 1970S, ALLERGAN WAS CONSIDERING A MERGER WITH A LARGE, RESEARCH-ORIENTED PHARMACEUTICAL COMPANY. "WHILE WE HAD BEEN SUCCESSFUL AS A PRODUCT-DEVELOPMENT COMPANY IN WHICH WE BASICALLY IN-LICENSED ACTIVE INGREDIENTS, WE DID NOT HAVE A TRUE RESEARCH CAPABILITY TO CREATE OUR OWN COMPOUNDS," GAVIN HERBERT EXPLAINS. "AS I LOOKED AHEAD, I THOUGHT IT NECESSARY TO HAVE THAT CAPABILITY."

Allergan welcomed the potential boost SmithKline would give the company's research capabilities. The merger and several acquisitions that followed helped Allergan enter new geographic markets and new product markets. Contact lens-care was a booming business and Allergan introduced the first multi-use sterile saline solution. Before long, Lens Plus was the largest selling product in its category.

SmithKline Beck
CORPO ION

An alliance seemed the best way to gain research capabilities. Allergan was approaching annual sales of $100 million. It was an attractive, growing firm that was already being pursued as an acquisition candidate. The Herbert family controlled about 35 percent of the stock (much of it in a trust), not enough to prevent a hostile takeover. The family and the trustees of the stock trust knew the company was attractive and decided a friendly merger was the best protection.

One of Allergan's suitors, a large Swiss firm, wanted to acquire the company for cash. "At that time tax rates on capital gains were approaching 70 percent," Gavin says. "Also, I was young enough that I wanted to continue running the business. So in response to the effort by the Swiss company, we began looking for a company that would be compatible and with potential for a stock deal, which was non-taxable."

SmithKline, rich with profits from its drug Tagamet, was actively looking at diversification and approached Allergan. "Allergan's position as the leading eye-care pharmaceutical company was attractive," says Henry Wendt, then president of SmithKline. "It had an entrepreneurial culture and a terrific record of growth in sales and profits. It seemed like a good fit, and we were anxious to add further elements to the business."

Herbert says, "When SmithKline approached us, I felt very comfortable with the management team there and their concept — to develop an eye-care business that embraced all of eye care and that would be managed here in California as a wholly owned subsidiary with my continuing to have the primary responsibility for managing the business." The directors agreed that a merger with SmithKline was in the best interest of the shareholders. "It certainly was not a step taken lightly," says Thomas O'Sullivan, a member of Allergan's board at the time. "It was an opportunity to have access to greater resources and research capabilities. Allergan would be a division of a company that had been a major force in the pharmaceutical business for a hundred years or more."

Discussions began in earnest toward the end of 1979, and the merger between Allergan and SmithKline became official on April 11, 1980, at a negotiated price of $260 million. "I was Gavin's new boss," Wendt says. "People in the industry who knew the two of us said this romance and marriage would last, at the most, six months, Gavin being a very independent, free-wheeling entrepreneurial type who had built this company. But Gavin went on the board of SmithKline, we worked very closely together, and the company continued to do extremely well under its new ownership." Allergan remained a division of SmithKline for the next nine years.

"I enjoyed an excellent relationship,"

SmithKline CEO Henry Wendt and Chairman Robert Dee, left to right, opposite, were instrumental in engineering the merger of SmithKline and Allergan. Allergan continued to operate as a nearly autonomous unit of SmithKline — or what became SmithKline Beckman following another merger in which Gavin Herbert would ironically play an instrumental role.

Gavin says. "I'd never worked for anybody else, but Henry Wendt was a good teacher. From my perspective, it worked out well." In addition to running Allergan, Gavin became president of SmithKline's eye- and skin-care products operations, and executive vice president of the parent company.

Gavin also brought some valuable connections. Not long after the merger, he introduced his friend, Arnold Beckman, to SmithKline CEO Henry Wendt and Chairman Robert Dee. SmithKline later acquired Beckman Instruments, becoming SmithKline Beckman.

Making the Merger Work

The Allergan management team remained virtually intact after the merger, and the company continued on much as it had before. SmithKline provided the company a key executive in Peter Ridley, who became Allergan's vice president for scientific development and set up the company's basic molecular research program. Gavin says Ridley "helped create the team that is an outstanding group with significant capabilities to create new and important chemical entities that will be a big part of our future growth." Lester J. Kaplan, with a doctorate in organic chemistry, joined Allergan in 1983 to help set up its chemistry group. That group's first program was retinoid research, an exciting field that promises compounds for the treatment of a variety of human ailments. "Having an integrated chemistry and biology research program is really the absolute fundamental for creating your own innovative drugs," Kaplan says. By the end of the decade, he was Allergan's vice president of research.

Although Allergan's growth bounded ahead through the whole period of the merger, the expected synergy between the two research and development departments did not happen. SmithKline was interested in drugs with a minimum potential of $100 million in annual sales. Even though Allergan was part of the same company, "we couldn't get on the SmithKline priority list," Gavin says. "Most of our products fell below that figure."

Wendt conceded that R&D collaboration "didn't work out as well as we'd hoped. We didn't discover any startling new ophthalmic super products. It's possible we didn't try hard enough, but it's not easy." SmithKline's R&D productivity lagged, and for several years, there was no important new product. Kaplan says no compounds or drugs came to Allergan from SmithKline that ever ended up in the marketplace. "It was a disappointment to those who had envisioned a synergy," he adds, "but on the other hand, with SmithKline support, I think we built a very strong, capable R&D department with a good discovery research program."

Bill Shepherd moved from vice president of operations to president of Allergan in 1984, working with Herbert, who continued as CEO, for the rest of the time Allergan and SmithKline were together. "My view of those nine years is neutral," he says. "There's good and bad. They gave us a lot of money to invest. At the same time, we were growing like crazy, so we were helping them tremendously. Some years we were 10 percent of their sales and a much higher percentage of their incremental growth. We did not get out of it what we hoped to get out of it in association with their research effort, but we had a tremendous run." During those nine years Allergan's annual sales zoomed from $100 million to more than $750 million.

Growth through Acquisitions

The company made several acquisitions during the merged period. One, in 1984, was Laboratoires Dulcis du Dr. Ferry, S.A., a French ophthalmic prescription drug firm. "The acquisition was minor — an ophthalmic specialty company," Gavin says, "but it was strategically important in building the French ethical pharmaceutical business. In France, it was difficult for foreign companies to register new products." Allergan had been courting the company for 10 years when the Dulcis chief, Christian Blanchet, confided to Gavin at an ophthalmic convention in Chicago that he'd received an offer from Nestle, parent of Allergan's rival, Alcon, and was inclined to accept it. Gavin sprang into action.

SmithKline had an elaborate system for acquisitions; a proposal had to go through several committees, and took months to get approval. That procedure would kill any possibility of a counteroffer from Allergan to Dulcis. Gavin appealed to Henry Wendt and Robert Dee to bypass the bureaucracy, and they agreed — if Herbert could bring Blanchet to company headquarters in Philadelphia. They provided him the corporate jet, and Gavin says he "kidnapped Christian and flew him to Philadelphia to meet the CEO and the board chairman. Within 24 hours, we'd made a deal."

In 1986, again with SmithKline's backing, Allergan acquired an American Hospital subsidiary, American Medical Optics, for $165 million. The firm, known as AMO, made intraocular lenses that ophthalmic surgeons implant to replace the eye's natural lens clouded by cataracts. As part of Allergan, AMO (now Allergan Medical Optics) has made spectacular advances, developing foldable, multifocal lenses that can be inserted through an incision so small it is self-sealing without stitches. Bob Bishop managed AMO for several years until he was given responsibility for Allergan's pharmaceutical business and then, in 1989, for corporate development and investor relations. Rich Ulmer then moved from president of pharmaceuticals to head of AMO. "The acquisition gave Allergan a chance to enter a part of the ophthalmic marketplace that it had never been in," Ulmer says. "I never had more fun in my 25 years with the company than going down to AMO. It was a tremendous experience."

ALLERGAN FRANCE

LABORATOIRES DULCIS: FROM HANDMADE TO HIGH PROFILE

For a busy Rx plant shipping 10 million units a year from a 30-product line, Laboratoires Dulcis is uniquely located, to say the least.

The offices and production facilities of one of France's oldest and best-known pharmaceutical firms are tucked into the western border of Monaco, the picturesque, four-square-mile playland on the breathtaking Mediterranean coast. In a tiny industrial sector of the famed principality, Dulcis occupies five floors in three office buildings.

Former Dulcis President Christian Blanchet recalls that it was his acquaintance with Allergan CEO Gavin Herbert through a prior licensing relationship (terminated in 1979) which led him to accept an offer from Allergan

Allergan's Rx business has historic roots in the picturesque playland of Monte Carlo. ▼

BUILDING DULCIS

Founded in France in 1907, Dulcis was moved to Monaco in 1935, and taken over by Blanchet's father, a pharmacist, in 1959.

"It was really a dying company," recalls Blanchet, who now serves as director of product licensing and acquisitions for Europe and reports to Allergan International President Dave Bruns. "We were only manufacturing some ointments, and this was done by hand, with 12 employees in 3,000 square feet under a bar in Monte Carlo, where the noise in the packaging room was mixed with noise from the slot machines upstairs. At that time, we were number six out of six companies in the market.

"My father began to relaunch the company," Blanchet continues. "He started to renew production and to get registration for new products—easier to get in those days. Then he started to rebuild the image

of the company, but there wa marketing or sales organizati

The elder Blanchet hired h to head up marketing and sal 1969, and by 1976, the sales had grown to five. In that yea Blanchet's father died sudden Blanchet became president a chairman of the board.

"That was a big challenge me," he admits. "I had just lo father, and I had about $1,00 my bank account, so I said, " we'll see what happens.' I wa marketing and sales people a pushing hard on existing pro When my father died in 197 were 5 million French francs by 1983, we were 27 million (US $5 million)."

1983 was a turning point f Dulcis. The firm received regi tions for four new products, a began feeling pressure from i national suitors.

"All these people were con to buy us," says Blanchet, "an question was, should we sell There were only four French vately owned companies in c at that time, and when POS, our toughest competitors, de to sell (to Alcon), I was finall convinced. It is always a mix

When it became clear that joining a multinational corporation would be desirable for Dulcis' future growth.

The acquisition of Laboratories Dulcis of France after a 10-year courtship was a huge international step enabling Allergan's entrance into major European markets that could be inhospitable to foreign companies seeking to register new products. Allergan consolidated the French operation from three towns into this single facility. Dulcis's founding (also in a drugstore) predates Allergan's, as this packaging suggests.

In 1979, before acquiring Allergan, SmithKline had bought Humphrey Instruments, which made computer-based ocular diagnostic devices. SmithKline assigned that business to Allergan after the merger, further broadening Allergan's eye-care niche. By 1986, that niche extended beyond pharmaceuticals, and the company changed its name from Allergan Pharmaceuticals to Allergan, Inc.

Getting into the contact-lens business had seemed a natural expansion for Allergan, but competitive shifts in that field began to trip up the company. Allergan's earlier strategy had been to work closely with lens makers in providing lens-care solutions for their products. Gavin uses the analogy, "You make the razor, we'll make the blades." Then its biggest partner in that arrangement, Bausch & Lomb, entered the solutions business. To stay competitive, Allergan decided it, too, had to make both the razor and the blades. The company bought International Hydron, a contact lens maker in 1985. An Allergan brochure sang a paean to the move: "Clearly the company is poised for a D-day in the contact-lens market. The addition of a lens company is a natural fit."

It turned out not to be. "The technology was emerging for disposable lenses," Gavin says, "and we were hopeful Hydron's technology would enable Allergan to get into the disposable-lens business. But we weren't successful at managing that business." Marketing lenses requires working closely with eye care professionals; the business is heavily service-oriented. "I don't think our sales people and marketing people really understood that it wasn't just selling the product," Gavin says. "In trying to integrate Hydron too fast, we lost a lot of the skills and a lot of the people who knew that service business. We also did not do a proper job on the manufacturing side of taking that core technology and expanding and investing in it."

Jackie Schiavo, corporate vice president, heads Allergan's production worldwide. She oversaw the transfer of Irvine manufacturing to a new facility in Waco, Texas, and some to Allergan's facility in Puerto Rico. Though the move caused some initial departures, an extensive internal and external placement effort made it a smooth transition.

Allergan ended up selling the contact-lens business. The U.S. business went to Ocular Sciences, and the European business became Hydron Europe, both of which were successful. "It was a tough lesson to learn," Gavin says. Henry Wendt said the two most controversial decisions during his involvement with Allergan were to get into the contact-lens business and to get out of the contact-lens business.

Important New Moves

Betagan, a beta blocker used in treating glaucoma, abnormal pressure in the eye, was one highly-successful example of in-licensing in the 1980s. The beta blocker had been developed by Warner-Lambert, and Allergan scientists saw the possibilities for treating glaucoma. Allergan licensed the rights to develop it for ophthalmology, formulated it into an eye drop, did the critical testing and regulatory requirements, and introduced the product internationally in 1985, and in the United States in 1986. It effectively lowered intraocular pressure in patients with open-angle glaucoma or ocular hypertension. Betagan also had the advantages of flexible dosage and multiple concentrations that allowed the medication to be prescribed to meet the individual patient's needs. It was the company's biggest drug for several years.

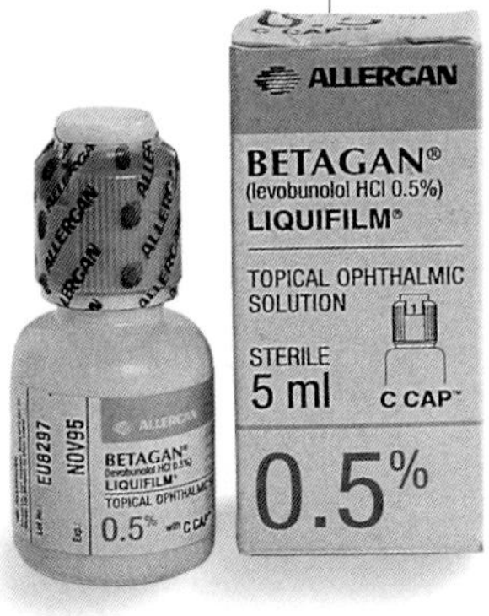

Betagan gave doctors the ability to precisely tailor glaucoma treatment for each patient.

To reduce costs in the face of

fierce competition, Allergan made a decision that was necessary but very difficult. In 1988, Allergan announced a plan to consolidate much of its manufacturing operations, a move that would affect some 220 Irvine employees. The plan was to gradually transfer contact-lens-care products manufacturing at the Irvine headquarters to a new plant in Waco, Texas, and all ophthalmic pharmaceuticals to Puerto Rico.

Expansion opportunity at the Irvine facility was limited, and the company had undertaken a year-long search to find a new manufacturing site. With tax incentives, available skilled labor and proximity to research universities, Waco emerged as a site where Allergan could expand its high-quality, low-cost manufacturing operations. The planned transfer would begin in 1989 and be completed by the third quarter of 1990. The transfer of prescription and over-the-counter products to the Puerto Rico facility was scheduled for completion by the end of 1990.

Allergan planned to continue production at Irvine until the transfer was complete and offered career counseling, job transfers and incentive packages to ease the transition. But employees who wished to stay in Irvine began leaving to find other jobs. Jackie Schiavo, then senior director of operations, was blunt about the problem in a statement for *Focus*, the company newsletter: "As we began losing employees, we realized that the original incentive package wasn't going to meet employees' or the company's needs. Morale and productivity are big issues. We have to balance the business need for quality products produced on time with the struggle to accept this shutdown. There's no way to candy-coat it; this plant is going away."

Allergan sought feedback on employee concerns through questionnaires and interviews and then came up with a policy that kept production going: retention bonuses for all affected employees and an extensive retraining and internal placement effort.

Botox Becomes a Winner

In the late 1980s, Allergan edged almost reluctantly into an acquisition and a product destined to be its biggest success ever. It developed from a most unlikely source — World War II research on possible weapons of biological warfare.

It's the most lethal toxin known to humans, but in the hands of skilled physicians, Botox (botulinum toxin type A) is remarkably safe and effective. In the 1970s, Alan Scott, an ophthalmologist at Smith-Kettlewell Eye Research Institute in San Francisco, found that tiny amounts of the toxin injected into eye muscles allowed close to normal muscle movement for patients with crossed eyes (strabismus). Also, injection into eyelid muscles restored functional vision for patients suffering from blepharospasm, an abnormal contraction of the eyelid muscles that can cause functional blindness. "Botox is injected, in extremely small amounts, directly into the muscle," says Les Kaplan. "The toxin doesn't travel very far from where it's injected, and there is very little exposure, so it can be administered safely."

Scott obtained an Investigational New Drug (IND) approval to treat those disorders with the toxin and did so successfully for years. Deciding it deserved wider use, he tried to get FDA approval on his own but was not successful. He asked Allergan to see it through FDA approval and to market it for his company, Oculinum Inc.

"We never really thought it was going to be a major product," Kaplan says. "There was not that much interest in actually doing it, to be honest." But researchers Steve Carlson and Judy Leon saw possibilities for the product in a range of conditions where there is abnormal muscle contraction. "They got me excited about it," Kaplan says. "Eventually we agreed to market it." Carlson in particular championed new indications for Botox, helping it develop to its full potential.

Rich Ulmer, who handled details of the marketing arrangement, says, "Scott's data were not adequate enough for FDA approval. So he gave us his data, we added our own clinical data, reorganized his work and showed that the product was safe and effective." It went on the market in 1989 under the name Oculinum, and new applications began developing.

The cosmetic use of Botox was inspired in 1987 when a patient in Canada was treated with Botox for blepharospasm and noticed that her brow furrow simultaneously improved. The ophthalmologist shared this information with her dermatologist husband, and the pair began using Botox on patients seeking a more youthful appearance. As their business grew, so did the interest of doctors elsewhere in using Botox for cosmetic purposes. Botox is in Phase II study for the treatment of brow furrow.

In 1991, Allergan bought Oculinum Inc., making Scott a wealthy man and giving Allergan full control of whatever new uses its research and development team would find for the drug. Allergan gave it the name Botox, and the drug became one of the highest selling products in Allergan's history, launching in 11 countries by the end of 1992.

James Cavanaugh and Peter Upton were responsible for implementing a five-year plan for international expansion in the early 1980s, and expansion in Europe was their top priority. Allergan consolidated the sales and marketing operations of its German subsidiary from multiple locations into a facility that was later sold. This modern building in Ettlingen, Germany, is the current headquarters of Allergan's German subsidiary.

International Growth

During the years as a division of SmithKline Beckman and beyond, Allergan's international business increased tenfold. Two key persons in the expansion were Peter Upton and James Cavanaugh, both of whom Gavin Herbert had recruited in 1977.

Cavanaugh, who has a doctorate in economics and health-care administration, had been a White House executive under Presidents Nixon and Ford. "I was attracted to the company because it was an emerging pharmaceutical company and it gave me the opportunity to learn the whole pharmaceutical business," Cavanaugh says. "Gavin assured me I'd get to see how it all worked." His first job was corporate planning, and he worked with other executives in writing a five-year plan for the company. Part of the plan was international expansion.

"We had an emerging international business," Cavanaugh says. "We had started a joint venture with a nearly century-old Japanese company, Santen, in the 1970s, and it was clicking along. We had a very profitable, good subsidiary in Germany. We had an emerging company in the United Kingdom. But most everything else was an export business. We needed to convert those into in-country businesses, especially in the major markets." To help develop an international strategy, he and Herbert persuaded Peter Upton, who had just retired from

U.K.-based Burroughs Wellcome, to join the company.

"International business was patchy," says Upton. "In many major markets, notably U.K., France and Italy, we had virtually nothing. However, we had developed a heavy involvement in South America despite

Cataracts No More

In times past, a person blinded by cataracts had just one possible treatment: a sharp blow to the head. The rap, if the patient was lucky, would displace the opaque lens in his eye, allowing light perception. "Couching" was the name given that primitive method of treatment.

Cataract treatment didn't advance much beyond couching until the twentieth century, when surgeons developed a way to remove the damaged lens. The method was to make a nearly semicircular incision in the eye, insert a cryoprobe behind the iris, freeze the crystalline lens, pluck it out as a complete unit, and tediously suture the cut with tiny, delicate stitches. Recovery was slow; sometimes it took as much as a year and a half for vision to stabilize. With no lens at all, the patient would be fitted with glasses that looked as thick as jar bottoms. Vision was distorted, but at least there was vision.

Today, with foldable intraocular lenses and phacoemulsification machines, an ophthalmic surgeon trained in the procedure makes a 2.5-millimeter incision (about the height of two pennies stacked), fills the eye with a viscous material to keep it inflated and prevent tissue damage and inserts a tip connected to a phaco machine. This breaks up the damaged lens with ultrasound and removes it like a tiny vacuum cleaner. The surgeon implants the new folded lens in the cavity where the natural lens had been and opens it inside the eye with another special tool, the Unfolder, rinses out the protective viscous material and the job is done. The incision is so small it may not require suturing; it is self-sealing.

An experienced surgeon can complete a cataract procedure in 15 to 30 minutes. "With the equipment and lenses, cataract surgery is really very successful and precise," says Patricia Knight, Allergan's vice president of research and development. There is virtually no trauma or recovery time; the patient doesn't even need an eye patch for the rest of the day.

Allergan's Unfolder instrument securely grips the folded intraocular lens and ensures precise placement in the eye.

the fact that each of the three European countries mentioned had a bigger market size than all the countries south of the Mexican border put together. There was an urgent need to change our market priorities." Rapid expansion in Europe was urgent because Allergan had established a new production facility in Westport, Ireland, and needed substantial new markets to fully utilize the new plant.

Upton, Cavanaugh and Herbert laid out a plan, and "country by country we started to build a business," Cavanaugh says. "The most positive thing that I found was the attitude of the staff," says Upton, "They were dedicated and hard-working." Allergan began with the U.K., sending Dave Berberian to get the market moving. He stayed five years and built up a business which was profitable in its first year.

Allergan bought an ophthalmologic specialty company in Italy and expanded it. "In France we recruited a fellow named Victor Ferreira," Cavanaugh says. "He and I found a little farmhouse outside of Strasbourg that had a barn behind it. We set up the barn as a warehouse and used the house as his office. We hired a sales person, and the business started to take off. In Australia Chris Greenhill had already built a very nice business for us. We had a really gung-ho team of people. They were entrepreneurial, they were business builders, they were loyal to what we were trying to do." Cavanaugh and Gavin Herbert agree that Ferreira was another of Allergan's entrepreneurial heroes. After building a business in France for the company, he transferred to Italy and increased Allergan's presence there. In a short span of time, both these countries, like the U.K., were making a profitable contribution to Allergan's international business.

Allergan set about creating a rational organization with the appointment of regional directors for Europe, the Pacific, South/Central America and distributor markets. Jon Thorsen, being an ophthalmologist, brought valuable technical expertise to the organization. "Allergan International received unstinting support from seasoned managers in the U.S. business," says Upton, "notably, Henry Glassner, vice president of sales in the United States, whose skills, wisdom and vast experience proved invaluable. It was Henry who allowed his most senior staff member, Rich Ulmer, to join us for a time as director of international marketing, where he made a great contribution."

Cavanaugh moved from Allergan in 1982 to head SmithKline's clinical laboratory business and then the pharmaceutical business. "Allergan was a superb training ground," he says. David Bruns, who had been Allergan's chief financial officer, succeeded Cavanaugh as vice president of international. "It was probably the best thing that ever happened to me in my life," Bruns says. "It was exciting. I was there from 1982 to 1992, and during that time we built the international business from about $40 million to about $450 million. It became a significant part of the company's sales and profit."

Initially, products for the care of contact lenses made up most of the European sales because they were not subject to government regulation or price controls. Allergan gradually won approval for pharmaceuticals, threading through requirements that differed from country to country. Bruns spoke of differences in medical practices as well as government regulations: "Even the use of products in northern Europe was entirely different from southern Europe because of cultural differences, the way people use medicines and the way doctors prescribe them." Bruns traveled more than half the time, keeping abreast of the varying needs of the international market.

By the end of the 1980s, Allergan had subsidiaries in 30 countries and was marketing products in more than 100. Sales outside the United States accounted for 54 percent of the company's business.

Standing Alone Again

Nine years after becoming a division of SmithKline, Allergan was spun out into an independent company with Gavin Herbert still in charge. It may be one of the few times in history that a firm has gone in and out of a years-long merger with the same CEO. Henry Wendt, who engineered both the merger and the spinoff, explains how it came about.

"I was negotiating what turned out to be the SmithKline-Beecham merger," he says. "It was a merger of equals in that the relative values and capitalizations would be very close. To balance that out, we spun out to the shareholders both Beckman and Allergan. I thought Allergan was perfectly capable of being an independent company again. It was much larger than it had been in 1979, and I knew it wouldn't be happy as part of the new merged company."

Gavin Herbert and Bill Shepherd set up a new board of directors for Allergan and invited three SmithKline directors, Wendt, William Grant and Handel Evans, to be members. The New York Stock Exchange once again began running the symbol AGN on June 21, 1989. "Both Allergan and

Beckman had been public companies," Gavin says. "The teams were pretty much still together. They hadn't scrambled the eggs. They were easily pulled apart in a rather short time."

There were many readjustments, however. "SmithKline was no longer our bank," Gavin says. "They'd provided us with quite a bit of funding for acquisitions and really hadn't charged us for the cost of that money. We had to re-educate the management team about return on investment and return on assets and the cost of money." The company tried to re-introduce the old Allergan culture to the much larger company it had become and to set up some of the old incentives, including stock options.

Allergan also faced a tough market. Contact-lens-care products accounted for nearly half its sales, and recently introduced disposable lenses and extended-wear lenses were cutting into that business. Henry Wendt talks about the problems Allergan faced: "The contact-lens-care market matured, so the principal market being served by the company slowed a lot. Allergan had diversified into the ophthalmic-instrument business [Humphrey Instruments], which proved to be a more difficult business than any of us had thought."

At about the same time, two major prescription drugs went off patent. Expenses went up several million dollars when the company assumed services SmithKline had provided for nine years: treasury, tax, investor relations, internal audit, external financial reporting, public affairs, human resources, legal and insurance.

Although the company grew by a few percentage points each year, sales, profits and stock prices sagged far below the expectations generated by decades of lively expansion. "We took our profits up too high in the 1980s," says Bill Shepherd, "and that's why we had trouble in the 1990s. We helped SmithKline, which is what a division should do, but I think in hindsight there was some pain to be paid in the 1990s by us. We had not been investing enough in the company in research or marketing or development of people." Rocks and shoals would litter Allergan's course for the next few years.

When the announcement came in 1989 that Allergan would spin off from SmithKline, rumors spread through Allergan that employees would have the afternoon off. The rumor was true. Allergan celebrated independence with an office picnic on the Irvine campus.

6 Independence

...to take arms against a sea of troubles... — *Hamlet,* William Shakespeare

At about the time Allergan became an independent company again, the pharmaceutical marketplace was changing dramatically. Health-care management organizations became fiercely competitive and harshly cost-conscious. The squeeze on what they would pay for drugs and services became ever tighter. By that time, a high percentage of doctors worked with Health Maintenance Organizations (HMOs), many of which demanded that they prescribe generic pharmaceuticals when available. Even more serious was the impact of Medicare rebates on the pharmaceutical industry.

No 3910296

THE UNITED STATES OF AMERICA

TO ALL TO WHOM THESE PRESENTS SHALL COME:

Whereas, there has been presented to the Commissioner of Patents and Trademarks a petition praying for the grant of Letters Patent for an alleged new and useful invention the title and description of which are contained in the specifications of which a copy is hereunto annexed and made a part hereof, and the various requirements of Law in such cases made and provided have been complied with, and the title thereto is, from the records of the Patent and Trademark Office in the Claimant(s) indicated in the said copy, and Whereas, upon due examination made, the said Claimant(s) is (are) adjudged to be entitled to a patent under the Law.

Now, therefore, these Letters Patent are to grant unto the said Claimant(s) and the successors, heirs or assigns of the said Claimant(s) for the term of Seventeen years from the date of this grant, subject to the payment of issue fees as provided by Law, the right to exclude others from making, using or selling the said Invention throughout the United States.

In testimony whereof I have hereunto set my hand and caused the seal of the Patent and Trademark Office to be affixed at the City of Washington this seventh day of October, in the year of our Lord one thousand nine hundred and seventy-five, and of the Independence of the United States of America the two hundredth

Attest: Attesting Officer

C. Marshall Dann, Commissioner of Patents and Trademarks

Gavin Herbert and Bill Shepherd together planned Allergan's future as an independent company. The marketplace was changing rapidly as U.S. Medicare rebates and generic competition placed new demands on pharmaceutical companies. Utilizing new technology to research and develop patented products became one of Allergan's chief objectives.

Retinoids was one productive area of research for Allergan. Rosh Chandraratna, head of Allergan's retinoids team, is known industrywide as the "father of retinoids." Internal research efforts and ventures crafted as funding vehicles helped make Allergan a leader in this field. Tazorac/Zorac is a product of Allergan's leading-edge receptor-selective research.

The government mandated 15 percent rebates for Medicare prescriptions of all drugs. Patents expired in the early 1990s on two of Allergan's major products, Betagan and Propine, opening them to generic copies. Nearly $100 million worth of annual sales disappeared.

"Starting in the late 1980s and into the 1990s, the world was changing," Bill Shepherd says. "You couldn't do things the way you'd done them before. You couldn't increase prices to make the bottom line. New marketing programs, more cost-effectiveness had to take place. If you did nothing in that environment you could be in big trouble. You had to try things."

Refocusing

Shepherd was president of Allergan at the beginning of the decade. Gavin Herbert had turned the presidency over to him in 1986 but continued as CEO until 1992. "Bill and I worked pretty well together," Gavin says. "He attended to inside things and was more detail-oriented. I tended to be Mr. Outside: things like interrelationships with other pharmaceutical companies or issues of the entire industry. I was on the executive committee of Pharmaceutical Research and Manufacturers of America (PhRMA), which represents the whole research-based pharmaceutical industry. In terms of strategy, Bill and I shared responsibility with the board."

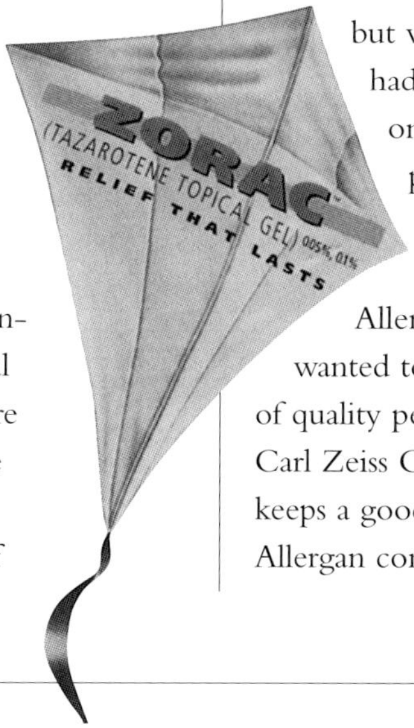

When Shepherd became CEO as well as president in 1992, Gavin continued as chairman. He officially retired in 1995, becoming chairman emeritus. ("Since 1996, I now have the luxury of doing just the fun things," he says.) Shepherd was elected board chairman. Richard Haugen, chief operating officer under Shepherd and who worked with both CEOs, said of their management styles, "Gavin was a visionary, marketing, creative individual. Bill was an operations-oriented, very objective, rational, hands-on, tactically oriented individual." Shepherd set to work refocusing Allergan's business.

One early move was the sale of the ophthalmic instruments business — Humphrey Instruments. "It's not in our area of expertise," Shepherd says. "We thought the business would do better under somebody else, but we were concerned because it had our name all over it." In fact, one Humphrey product line — phacoemulsification machines, basic to modern cataract surgery — was designed by Allergan engineers. "We very much wanted to put the company in the hands of quality people." Allergan made the sale to Carl Zeiss Co. in November of 1991 but keeps a good relationship with Humphrey. Allergan continues designing new phaco machine models and Humphrey began building all of the models for the company again in 1999.

Another cost-effective move that worked well was what Jackie Schiavo, now vice president for worldwide operations, called globalization. Beginning in 1991, Allergan began consolidating its manufacturing operations, reducing the number from more than 15 to basically five. "This is a place where Allergan can be proud," Schiavo says, "because I think organizationally we're way ahead. We're at a place with our manufacturing network that truthfully many companies desire to be.... The model has subsequently been adopted by other companies. They're finding they can't afford the proliferation of plants." Allergan closed plants gradually and only after giving notice of six months or more.

In the early 1990s, Bill Shepherd directed a strategic change, with the aim of making Allergan a company driven by technology. "The company had technology," he says, "but it was not a strategy. This was a market-driven company up until then." Technology was the force needed to develop new products, the main weapon against generics and the only way to further Allergan's mission of making ever-better medicines.

But the strategic change, the plant consolidations and a later management restructuring required what Shepherd described as "huge" layoffs. Anyone who pictures management as being coldly indifferent to the pain of layoffs should talk to Bill Shepherd.

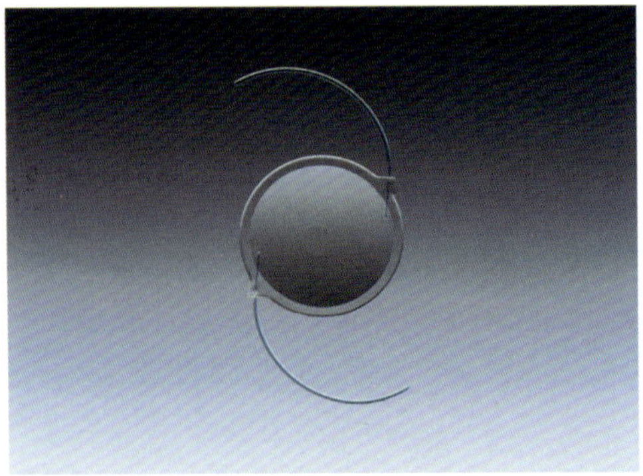

Allergan's intraocular lenses (IOLs) are foldable, allowing surgeons to insert them through very small incisions. The protruding loops, called haptics, work like springs to hold the lens centered in place.

When he was asked years later about staff cuts, his face seemed to crumple for a moment and he said softly, "That's awful; it's awful." But then he added, "As CEO of a company with 6,000 people, you have a responsibility for all of them. If you've got to let 500 go to save the other 5,500, you do that. Does it make it any less painful? Hell no." Haugen had his own job eliminated in the management restructuring, but he calls it "just part of business life in the last five to ten years. It was difficult, but I was part of the process, and I totally agreed with what we went through for the business to maintain a healthy status. It was painful but totally appropriate."

Retinoid Research

The man called "the father of retinoids," Rosh Chandraratna, joined Allergan in 1984 to help establish the program. "We had a very simple goal which was to make a topical retinoid that will work in acne," he recalls. Retinoids are chemical messengers that bind to receptor sites in cells, regulating a broad range of biological functions. Among these functions are cell proliferation and differentiation, lipid metabolism and immune function.

There are six known retinoid receptors, divided into two families—the Retinoic Acid Receptors (RARs) and the Retinoid X Receptors (RXRs). Within each family, there are three subtypes—alpha, beta and gamma. Each individual receptor appears to have distinct biological functions. To date, the use of retinoids has been limited by toxic side effects. These side effects are attributable to the non-selective nature of the compounds. By activating all of the retinoid receptors, they achieve not only the desired effect but also undesirable side effects. For example, virtually everyone who takes Accutane, the oral medication for acne, develops mucotaneous toxicities, such as irritations of the lips or nose.

What sets Allergan's retinoid effort apart is the research group's commitment to developing receptor-selective retinoids. These compounds target only select receptors in an effort to reduce side effects. "Our compounds may not work in the same breadth of diseases as non-selective compounds," says Rosh Chandraratna, "but in the diseases where they do work, they will have fewer toxic side effects." Rather than aiming for a one-retinoid-fits-all product, Chandraratna's team is researching and developing a variety of receptor-selective retinoids, tailored to specific disease applications.

Allergan found new ways to finance this new research, forming a joint venture in 1992 with Ligand Pharmaceuticals for research on retinoids. The collaboration progressed into a joint company in 1994, Allergan Ligand Retinoid Therapeutics, Inc., shortened to ALRT. Rosh Chandraratna, Allergan's principal retinoid researcher, proposed the collaboration as well as an increased staff "if you really want to exploit the potential of these compounds." Important compounds came from that partnership including a retinoid for Type II diabetes with promise as a treatment for diabetes that was licensed to Warner Lambert.

The two companies discontinued ALRT in 1998 after a successful run and divided its compounds and research data. Allergan then formed a public research company with a contribution of $200 million, Allergan Specialty Therapeutics, Inc., (ASTI) to continue research on retinoid and neuroprotective technology.

Although short-lived, the profound importance of Allergan's joint venture with Ligand was memorialized by inclusion in Recombinant Capital's listing of the "Ten Deals that Changed Biotech" — the Allergan/Ligand agreement was listed as #5.

The investment in basic retinoid research Allergan began in the 1980s began to pay off in the 1990s with the introduction of a retinoid product for psoriasis marketed under the names Tazorac and Zorac. It was the first product Allergan developed from molecule to market, in-house, and just what Chandraratna was looking for. The basic ingredient Allergan researchers built was tazarotene, a new chemical entity. Chandraratna says, "It was kind of a

watershed point in our history because we started the basic drug discovery research program at Allergan, proving that we can take a drug from concept to marketing."

Vision Restored

The acquisition of AMO, the intraocular lens maker, in 1986 also was proving a good fit for Allergan in the 1990s. In 1989, the company introduced a silicone intraocular lens called PhacoFlex that folded to permit insertion through a small incision, the first of its kind. Research continued toward developing an even thinner material for an even smaller incision. Allergan introduced its second-generation foldable lens, the PhacoFlex II, in 1993, and within a year, it had become the best-selling intraocular lens in the world. Thinner than its predecessor, it was offered in a variety of powers.

The latest intraocular lens, the Array, introduced first in Europe and then in the U.S., is multifocal, allowing the patient close, medium and distant viewing. It accomplishes that with a series of concentric rings of varying refractions. All the images are transmitted to the eye at once, which sounds like a design for utter confusion. But that most astonishing of all computers, the human brain, sorts out the images, focusing on what the user is looking at, whether it's a want ad, a companion or a sunset. When multifocal lenses are implanted in both eyes, the patient can often retire his glasses. Paul Ernest, a surgeon from Michigan, recalls, "Patients were demanding second eye surgery immediately.

When Allergan achieved $1 billion in sales in 1995, the milestone was celebrated in grand style. Allergan employees came from all over the world to a gala celebration under a tent in Irvine. Flags displayed at the celebration and a special logo Allergan created for the event stressed the key role international expansion played in attaining this goal.

They would begin to cry because they could see so beautifully on the first day."

Val Portney, was the project leader of the multifocal-lens research and development. Patricia Knight, who has a doctorate in biomedical engineering, came to Allergan with the acquisition of AMO and now is vice president, research and development, overseeing intraocular-lens (IOL) projects. She calls the Array Allergan's "ultimate lens." A person nearly blinded by cataracts gains the vision young, healthy eyes provide when multifocal lenses are implanted, she says. She explains that it's "pseudo-accommodation." Natural accommodation is when the crystalline lens actually changes shape. But patients are better off than they were even before they had cataracts, because now they can see both near and far without glasses. So it is kind of like young eyes, in a sense." Surgeon Hiroko Bissen-Miyajima of Japan agrees: "All patients expressed satisfaction with their surgical results. The Array can provide quite a high level of quality of life."

The devices surgeons use in the implant procedure are called phacoemulsification machines. (Phaco refers to the crystalline lens.) Allergan has designed and engineered three models, the Diplomax, the Prestige and the Sovereign, which are built for the company by Humphrey Instruments. They are sophisticated machines the surgeon can program for his particular technique and that allow him to complete cataract surgery in minutes with a minimum of trauma to the eye. Ivan Marais, a surgeon from South Africa says, "Foldable lenses allowed me to change my technique, and the benefits were manifold. Self-sealing wounds led to cataract surgery becoming an outpatient procedure. Patients could have good vision from day one." A cataract patient can enter surgery late in the morning and be home for lunch with a new vision of the world. Allergan has trained several thousand surgeons worldwide in the use of its phaco equipment. "My colleagues were quickly won over by this new technique," says surgeon Paul Turut of France.

Technology was critical not just to Allergan's research program but also to the efficient running of the company. With electronics developing faster than weeds after a spring rain, Allergan improved its computer technology enormously in the decade. In 1993, the company established a system called the Allergan Computer Architecture Project, dubbed ACAP. It was a worldwide network of databases replacing the mainframe computer in Irvine that stored marketing, accounting, personnel and financial data.

Later in the decade, the company advanced another step in data processing by installing Systems Applications and

been about 300 marketing class-action settlements, Barillas is

Allergan Gets OK to Market Ocuflox

IRVINE—Allergan Inc. said Tuesday that it has received U.S. Food and Drug Administration marketing clearance for its Ocuflox solution. Ocuflox is a topical anti-infective agent for bacteria that cause inflammation of membranes surrounding the eye. The company said it plans to launch Ocuflox in America by the end of the year.

The company said it currently sells the solution in Australia, Brazil, France, Greece, Italy, South Africa and the United Kingdom; approval in Canada and Spain is pending.

The company's stock rose 12.5 cents Tuesday to close at $22.625 on the New York Stock Exchange.

Ocuflox, an anti-infective for bacterial conjunctivitis, was just one new product that boosted Allergan's sales and its stock price in the late 1990s. Acular, a treatment for ocular itching; Complete, a one-bottle lens-care solution; and Alphagan, a revolutionary treatment for glaucoma, all put to rest doubts about Allergan's ability to face the competition of the 1990s.

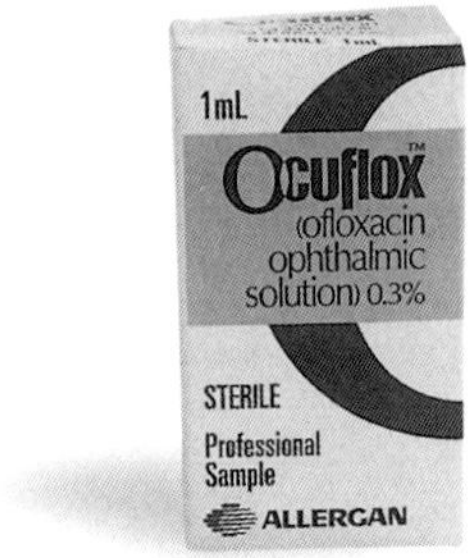

Programming (SAP), which replaces several Allergan programs, including ACAP. All of Allergan's manufacturing, commercial and R&D sites around the world share information using common, consistent formats. SAP provides instant global communication of Allergan's enormous store of data ranging from the profile of an ophthalmologist in Tokyo to the number of Botox vials on hand in Westport, Ireland.

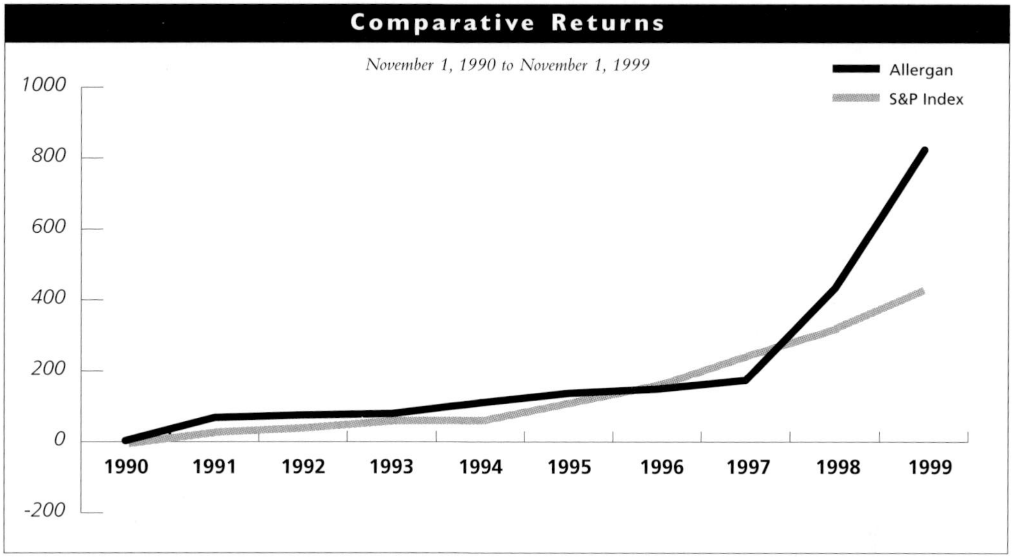

Justified Progress

Allergan scored two notable legal triumphs during the 1990s. The company was vindicated in 1993 when a U.S. District Court judge dismissed a shareholder lawsuit brought against it in 1989. A law firm specializing in what Gavin Herbert describes as blackmail had filed the action, claiming the company did not achieve the earnings it had forecast. Most companies settle such suits rather than go to court, but Gavin and Bill Shepherd decided to fight.

"We had a history of growing at 20 percent a year," Gavin says, "and it was obvious we couldn't keep doing that forever, although we'd been doing it for 25 years. I tried to lower expectations by saying I thought mid-teens growth was an achievable objective. Growth ended up being 8 or 10 percent." One dip in the stock price was all it took to trigger the suit the law firm had already prepared. "The legal battle dragged on for a couple of years and cost us a ton of money, but I'm glad we fought it until the suit was dismissed," Gavin says. "Giving in to that kind of blackmail was unacceptable to us."

The 1990s also marked the largest patent-dispute settlement in Allergan history. The company defended its patent on foldable intraocular lenses against infringement and finally was offered a satisfactory license fee and royalties. Martin Voet, the company's chief patent counsel, said, "We can't say we won, because it was settled, but basically I think you win when the other side agrees to pay you lots of money, which is what happened. I like to remind people that 1997 was the year the legal department became a profit center!"

Despite somewhat disappointing performance in the first half of the 1990s decade, Allergan achieved a significant goal in 1995: Sales topped a billion dollars for the first time. Allergan employees all over the world celebrated the milestone with parties, including a gala affair in Irvine that featured music by The Temptations.

A significant Allergan product that boosted sales in the late 1990s was Alphagan (introduced in 1996), a new concept for treating glaucoma. Alphagan quickly became the largest-selling Allergan ophthalmology product. Other products sparking the market were Acular (introduced in 1993), to relieve ocular itching; Ocuflox (introduced in 1993), an anti-infective agent for bacterial conjunctivitis; and Complete (introduced in 1994), a one-bottle lens-care solution.

International Opportunities

Allergan made a significant push throughout the decade to get more of these products to more customers around the globe. Sensitivity to the cultural differences that Upton and Cavanaugh had identified a decade ago remained the focus of Allergan's marketing approach.

Jim Mazzo, who joined Allergan as a sales representative in 1980 and became president for Europe, Africa and the Middle East in 1998, says the differences have persisted despite the European common market. "One of the first things you have to do is realize that you must specialize by country," he says. He uses what he calls "passive listening" to sense culture nuances. "When I'm in Italy, I'm speaking to an Italian and understanding that his or her needs are a bit

The Alphagan Story

Diligence is the mother of good fortune. — *Miguel de Cervantes*

Allergan has gone through the FDA approval process with countless drugs. As a matter of fact, some 25 to 30 compounds are in various phases of testing at almost any given moment. Which ones will fall by the wayside and which ones will see commercial success? There's no way to predict, but the story of one of Allergan' successes, traced from the beginning of the process to the end, demonstrates the difficult task Allergan faces. Our choice is Alphagan, the company's most popular prescription drug.

The process started in the mid-1980s, when Allergan was studying a chemical called brimonidine and its potential to treat glaucoma. Glaucoma is abnormal pressure of fluid in the eye, which damages retinal ganglion cells. "This is the cell that's kind of the cable between the eye and the brain," says Les Kaplan, Allergan's president of research and development. "With increased pressure in the eye, the retinal ganglion cells that make up the optic nerve die off, and one slowly loses vision."

The eye, he says, is somewhat like a pond with a faucet bringing liquid in and a drain taking it out: "If you put more liquid in the eye than you drain out, pressure increases. To lower pressure you can either decrease the amount of fluid that enters the eye or increase the amount that exits the eye. Beta blockers [the most efficacious drugs before Alphagan] limit the fluid coming into the eye, but they can cause serious problems for people with pulmonary disease. Alphagan [part of a compound class known as alpha2 agonists] works on both sides of the equation, lowering the inflow and increasing the outflow. It does not have any effect on the pulmonary system and has a much lower effect on the heart."

With the goal of producing such a drug, Kaplan and his researchers in the mid-1980s began what became a 10-year, $45-million quest. A literature search found that pharmaceutical giant Pfizer owned the molecule patent for brimonidine. Pfizer's laboratory in Sandwich, England, had studied it as a potential drug to lower blood pressure. Pfizer tried to develop it into a systemic hypertensive agent but failed because the compound has a very short systemic effect once it goes into circulation. The quick loss of efficacy is problematic for a systemic drug, but Allergan saw a glimmer of hope that it could work as an ophthalmic drug.

A University of Texas scientist, David Potter, had been studying the compound when Allergan hired him in the 1980s. Potter's experiments looked promising, and Allergan decided to seek a licensing agreement with Pfizer. Through Gavin Herbert's friendly relationship with Pfizer, Allergan got not only the license, but Pfizer's data package, representing at least two years of research.

But there was a problem: One of Pfizer's animal trials showed an unwanted side effect. Was it an anomaly? "That was a critical point," Kaplan says. "Big red flag. We convened an expert panel to review the data." The panel's recommendation: The side effect was most likely an anomaly, but Allergan probably should repeat the study. "These are two-year, multi-million-dollar studies," Kaplan says. "We really didn't want to repeat, but we made the decision to redo it. After taking the time and spending the money, we found that the side effect actually was an anomaly. The new studies came out clean."

Next came human testing. "It looked extremely promising after the first test," says Kaplan, "so we proceeded with the next step, the multi-dose process." The phase III studies included about a thousand people, who received treatment for six months to a year. Alphagan proved to be safe and efficacious. Allergan submitted a New Drug Application thousands of pages long to the FDA in the fall of 1995. The FDA response was favorable, but the agency insisted that Alphagan be labeled a three-times-a-day drug. Allergan's research indicated twice a day produced good results, but the FDA wouldn't budge.

Despite the three-times-a-day labeling setback, Allergan's strategic marketing group forged ahead. Prior to launching the drug, Allergan's U.S. marketing and training teams prepared sales representatives over a two-year period in area training sessions, by computer communication and in sessions with practicing ophthalmologists. Company researchers even tested the name: Did it translate well in all major languages? Was it easy to remember? The company asked hundreds of doctors for their reactions to the clinical research findings. A two-and-a-half-day sales meeting in Lake Geneva, Wisconsin, culminated the marketing preparations.

The FDA gave Alphagan final approval September 6, 1996, and Allergan began shipping the product to U.S. wholesalers on October 1. A telephone-sales force introduced Alphagan to more than 17,000 ophthalmologists. The official U.S. launch came at the American Academy of Ophthalmology meeting in Chicago the last week of October. Allergan people manning the company's booth in the exhibition hall were inundated by physicians asking about Alphagan and requesting samples for their offices. A two-year campaign began to introduce the drug to world markets.

Alphagan went on the market with modest expectations — perhaps $50 million in annual sales at its peak. As of the summer of 1999, annual sales were approaching $200 million, and millions of glaucoma patients see a brighter future than they'd ever imagined.

different from a Spaniard's," he says. His sales representatives are natives not only of the countries they serve but of the region because "a person from Sicily would have a very difficult time in Naples."

Competition abroad in the 1990s was just as tough or tougher than in the U.S. The introduction of disposable lenses flattened the market for lens-care products in Europe as well as the United States, Mazzo said, but he's upbeat. "People are now moving into a new contact-lens modality called frequent replacement. This type of program offers the patients and practitioners a new opportunity for lenses and solutions." The pharmaceutical industry in many countries requires that sales reps have a degree in science, Mazzo says, "so the representatives in most of the countries are looked upon as somebody who's well educated. They're expected to provide more information.

"Overall, the European market offers some distinctive advantages for many companies in that you are able to launch new products/indications earlier than in the U.S. market. We have had very positive experiences, most recently with our Sensar acrylic IOL as well as receiving new indications for Botox."

In Asia Pacific, the lens market is behind the rest of the world, and the introduction of disposable lenses has had less impact in the Asia Pacific region, according to Dave Fellows, Allergan's president for that region. "Some consumers in Asia don't like the idea of throwing away a perfectly good lens," he says. "It seems wasteful, particularly in a region where people can't afford to waste things. Disposable lenses have been slower to take hold, but they are coming."

In fact, Japan became one of Allergan's strongest foreign markets in the 1990s. The joint venture with Santen that had started in the 1970s to market contact-lens-care products thrived. But Allergan later launched three other businesses in Japan that ran into difficulties at about the time Allergan became an independent company again. Ted Danse, who headed the company's Latin American business, was transferred to Japan in 1990 to restore order. He said he found a variety of problems. A product recall of intraocular lenses had caused the company to lose face in Japan for that business. Allergan's contact-lens business in Japan was in trouble. Even the lens-care business, while still profitable, was losing market share.

"I put together a strategy called the Genesis Plan to grow the business for Allergan in Japan over 10 years," Danse says. "The executive committee approved the plan, and we went forward with it. To the credit of Bill Shepherd and everyone else, there was a lot of support. There really was a desire to plant the flag in Japan and grow there. By investing appropriately, we built up the surgical business so that it really was a leader in the area."

In 1996, Allergan bought out Santen's half of the joint venture. Allergan had already acquired the lens-care business of Pilkington Barnes-Hind, which included a soft-lens disinfectant, Consept F, that was popular in Japan. The company's total annual sales in Japan had reached about $100 million by the end of the decade. Allergan had sold both Humphrey and Hydron (contact lenses) by then and was concentrating on lens-care products, surgical products and pharmaceuticals.

The Japanese pharmaceutical market differs from other markets in that Japanese physicians dispense and sell medications. Large numbers of sales representatives call on doctors with a much higher frequency than elsewhere, so each rep services fewer doctors. Japan has a price-control system that allows an initial higher price for a new drug but cuts that price substantially each subsequent year.

In April 1997, Botox became the first and only prescription drug Allergan sells directly in Japan. It took the company six years of preparation to gain technical and reimbursement approval for Botox from the Japanese Ministry of Health and Welfare (MHW). Approval of prescription drugs is complicated and difficult for a foreign company to attain without a Japanese partner. Pharmaceuticals are still a small percentage of the company's business there.

The company has a large surgical business in Japan, and Dave Fellows keeps Allergan a strong participant in Asian ophthalmic conventions. At one conference Allergan conducted "The Unfolder Challenge." Physicians were invited to insert a folded silicone intraocular lens into an eye mock-up through an incision of less than 3 millimeters using Allergan's special "Unfolder" technology. A skilled surgeon walked them through the process and then let each try it. More than 300 did. "Japanese ophthalmologists love that type of program," Fellows says. "It's a specific challenge to their skill, and it was very well accepted." Today Japan is Allergan surgical's second-largest market next to the U.S., thanks to well-trained and aggressive sales team.

Japan has been Allergan's largest Asian market through the years, but the company undertook other successful ventures in Asia during the 1990s. In 1994, the company formed a joint venture with Nicholas Piramal India Limited to market a range of prescription ophthalmic products of both companies and contact-lens-care products. Under the agreement, the Indian firm Nicholas Piramal manufactures Allergan's products and transfers them to Allergan, which in turn sells to the end-user. "What they brought to the party is low-cost manufacturing capability which we otherwise would have had to invest in," Fellows says. When the two-company arrangement was announced, Ajay Piramal, chairman of Nicholas Piramal, released a statement that said, "This joint venture with Allergan will help bring high-technology eye-care products to India where some 20 million people suffer from cataracts."

Marketing in India included selling new, high-tech pharmaceutical products to Indians who can afford them and a broad line of generic products made for Allergan by Nicholas Piramal to those with humble incomes. Fellows says that method has proved to be an effective model for any developing market. Most physicians in India welcome sales representatives, Fellows says: "They know the reps will give them access to the most recently developed products, so they want to see the rep on a regular basis. It's a way for them to feel they're getting the latest information and products in ophthalmology." Allergan is the #1 ophthalmic company in India after only four years in operation.

A major problem in the Asia Pacific region is retaining highly skilled employees. "Allergan has an exceptional reputation for quality training," Fellows says, "so we're targeted by other companies. It's much easier

Jinwu Shi, vice mayor, spoke at the official ribbon-cutting ceremony in Hangzhou marking the beginning of Allergan's trade with China. There are currently 45 employees in this plant, one of the most technologically advanced in China.

to increase someone's salary than to invest in a training program for new hires. So keeping key people and hiring quality people are big challenges."

In 1997 and 1998, the company built a $30 million sterile ophthalmic products plant in China to manufacture for the entire Asia Pacific region, including Australia. The city in which it is located, Hangzhou, has special meaning for Gavin Herbert. In 1982, he was in China with Richard Nixon on the 10th anniversary of the Shanghai Communique. "One of the places we visited was Hangzhou, kind of the garden city of China," Gavin says. "It was built on an artificial lake created in the twelfth century, so of course for me it was an intriguingly beautiful place. Much of the Shanghai Communique was negotiated with Chou En-lai in his summer home there." Herbert stayed out of the site selection by company executives but was delighted when they chose Hangzhou for the plant. Today, Allergan is manufacturing Complete lens-care solution for a number of Asian countries there and will begin producing a full range of pharmaceutical products in 2000.

In the mid-1990s, Allergan's presence in Latin America also grew. Allergan had acquired LOA, a pharmaceutical company in Argentina, in 1992. And in 1995, Allergan increased its presence in Latin America with the acquisition of Laboratorios Frumtost SA, Brazil's largest manufacturer of eye-care pharmaceuticals. Frenzied economic fluctuations, however, make Latin America "a very tough part of the world to do business in," says Ted Danse who headed that market for a time. "The challenge with Latin America has always been that if you have invested in lots of assets, you have lots of exposure when the economy falls out." Allergan remained committed to this market during the 1990s, however, and Brazil quickly became the company's third-largest national market.

Educating the Customer

Cataract

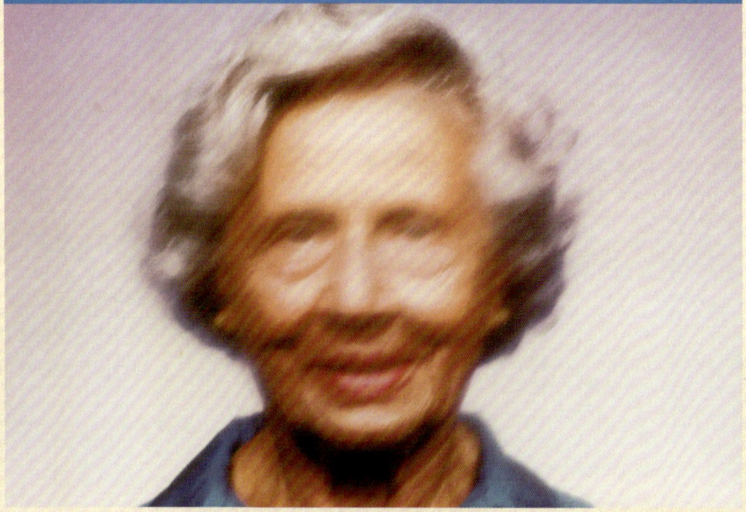

Glaucoma

Retinal Detachment

Strabismus

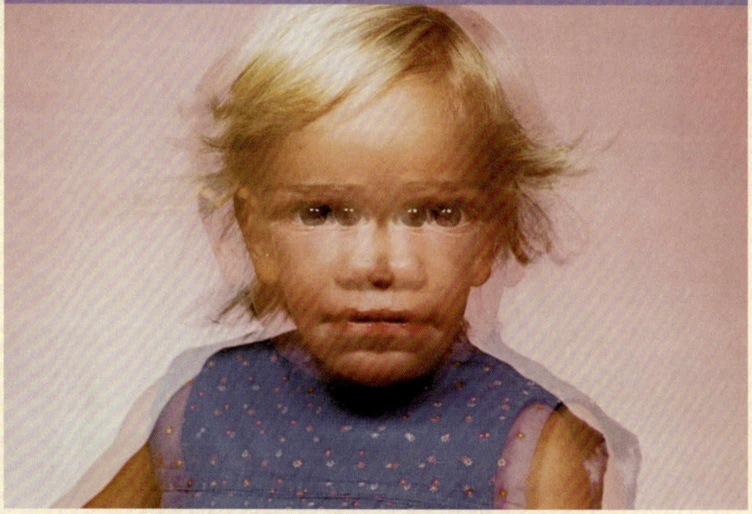

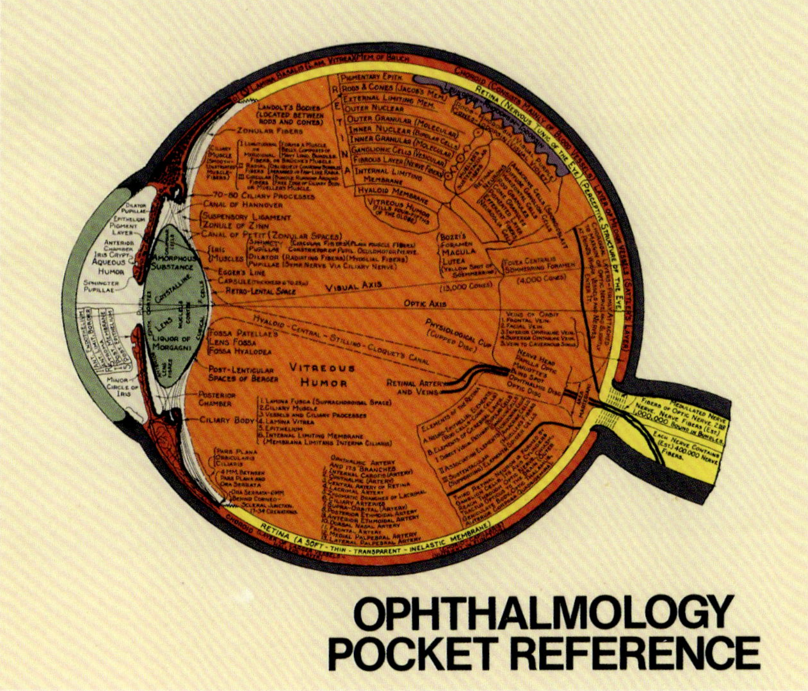

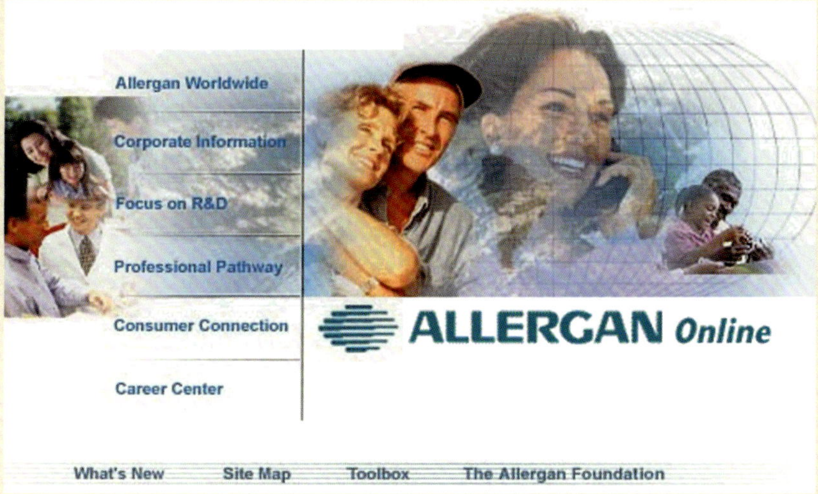

Educating the public has always been important to Allergan. The four posters at left were part of a series that ophthalmologists used extensively in the 1970s to explain various vision disorders. A version of the pocket reference, above, top, was produced as a poster during these same years. Such facts and descriptions are even more in demand in today's information age, and the Internet is a key tool for distributing them.

EuroCentre Comes On Line

Allergan also initiated centralized order taking and billing for Europe with a special unit in Dublin called the EuroCentre. The process began in 1997, when France's customer service operations were moved, and ended in 1999 with the inclusion of Italy. "Just think of all the complexities that went into harmonizing across all the countries," says Arno Habicht, director of the EuroCentre. "Dedicated Allergan employees made it all work. From a customer perspective, our goal to centralize customer operations has been to make it as seamless as possible."

If customers in France, Italy or South Africa phone Allergan, they dial a toll-free number in their own country but are connected automatically to the EuroCentre. There, an international team responds to customers from about 15 different countries in a dozen different languages. When a customer initiates a call to Allergan, that customer's profile flashes instantly on a computer screen at the EuroCentre. A multilingual operator answers the call, carefully using the correct dialect.

Jim Mazzo describes how it works: "If, say, an Austrian calls in and a German answers the phone, he even has to be careful how he 'Hello' because the language is a bit different in each country. Say it the wrong way, and the customer could be offended."

When the EuroCentre was new, a conscientious operator tried to make a customer from far away feel as if he was talking to a fellow countryman. The customer commented on "what beautiful weather we're having." "Yes it is beautiful," the operator responded, looking through the window at cold rain falling from the gray Dublin sky.

In July 1999, Allergan's board of directors met in Westport, in part to experience EuroCentre operations first hand. Above, Norbert Bensalem, far left, customer service manager, explains telephone techniques to, left to right, Herbert Boyer, Henry Wendt and Frank Tunney. At left, Credit Control Manager Joan Casey speaks with, left to right, Frank Tunney, Henry Wendt, EuroCentre Operations Director David Flynn and Herbert Boyer.

As of June 1999, all European, African and Middle Eastern markets are now combined into one at the EuroCentre, serving approximately 40,000 customers. "This integration of the business has given Allergan a significant competitive advantage," says David Flynn, operations director of the EuroCentre. "Since the introduction of this centrally-managed system, everyone has been able to focus attention on customers' orders and needs." Arno Habicht says, "the biggest advantage is that customers get better technical support."

In July 1999, the Allergan board gathered in Ireland to meet and review the operation in Westport, as well as the EuroCentre. The Allergan investment in the Ireland plant and the EuroCentre in 1999 exceeds $100 million and the plant now occupies 450,000 square feet, making it the largest Allergan production facility in the world.

Allergan has also invested in the Westport area. In 1987, when the company first came to town, it decided to help the town purchase land upon which a park could be built. Twelve years later, a new Leisure Centre has been completed. Council Manager Padraig Hughes speaks proudly of the new Leisure Centre, which has a 25-meter swimming pool, a children's pool, a fitness suite, health spa, plunge pool, aerobic studio and an auditorium with 150 retractable seats. He says, "It received funding approval from the European Union after we were able to show that we had a suitable site for it. Such a site would not have been available, but for Allergan's commitment, in partnership with the Town Council and the Department of the Environment, to invest in a town park in Westport in 1987. And for that we will always be grateful."

The company is also fortunate that a new, four-star hotel has been built in Westport, literally across the street from the plant. The Knockranny House Hotel was the venue for Allergan's board of directors for their July 1999 meeting. This magnificent four-star hotel, ably managed by Geraldine and Adrian Noonan, sits on an elevated site overlooking the town and has panoramic views of mountains and sea.

Marketing Changes

Changes in the marketplace and in the way people communicate dictated a rapid evolution of Allergan's marketing strategies. Handel Evans, an Allergan board member and a consultant to the pharmaceutical industry, said direct-to-consumer advertising by pharmaceutical companies had reached $1.333 billion dollars in the United States as of 1997, "and it's growing by leaps and bounds. It's to make the consumer aware of availability and seek the doctor's advice on whether or not a specific product is appropriate — unlike our generation, which took what the doctor gave them. I think that's a huge change."

Michael Ball, corporate vice president, says the company began advertising directly to consumers in the U.S. with a 1999 campaign called the Cataract Awareness Program. Advertisements in several national magazines are targeted at elderly people "to help them identify whether or not they could potentially have a cataract and urge them to go to their physician to ensure that they're doing all they can to protect their eyesight," Ball says. "We have a number of options they may want to discuss with their physician, and one is the Array multifocal lens. Obviously the physician makes the ultimate decision, but the idea is to help seniors identify potential problems and treatments."

Allergan also promotes some products on the Internet. "The Internet is creating a sea change in health care by providing patients with access to detailed information," Evans says. "The most recent statistics show that health is the number one hit on the Internet."

Looking for a Leader

In 1997 Bill Shepherd told the board he would retire at the end of the year. "I think I was feeling the stress," he says. "I was traveling 120 days a year. I had blessed every decision this company made from 1984 on, and I thought one day, 'Fourteen years is enough.' I have no regrets."

Shepherd's position as board chairman went to Herbert W. Boyer, whom Shepherd had recruited as a board member in 1994. Boyer is a distinguished biochemist, a former professor at the University of California at San Francisco, co-founder of Genentech, Inc., and recipient of several awards for research. Shepherd and the board embarked on an international search to choose a new CEO.

"We put as the number one objective a strong leader," board member Henry Wendt says, "and as number two, marketing savvy; number three, a record of performance in the health-care industry; and number four, a grasp of research and development." Handel Evans, also a board member, added to the criteria "someone with the right credentials from an educational point of view and who had lived abroad — someone who would treat the business as though it were his own." They found the fit in David Pyott.

7 Allergan at the Millennium

Lend me the stone strength of the past and I will lend you the wings of the future, for I have them. — Robinson Jeffers

ALLERGAN'S FUTURE BEGINS IN ITS RECENT PAST — 1998 TO BE EXACT, WHEN DAVID PYOTT SET IN MOTION THE SWEEPING CHANGES THAT WILL SHAPE THE COMPANY IN THE NEW MILLENNIUM. IN PYOTT'S FIRST YEAR ALONE, ALLERGAN'S STOCK PRICE NEARLY DOUBLED, REFLECTING WALL STREET'S CONFIDENCE IN THE NEW ALLERGAN. "IN THE SPORTS WORLD, DAVID WOULD BE KNOWN AS A PHENOM," SAYS HERBERT W. BOYER, CHAIRMAN OF THE BOARD. "HE HAD KEEN INSIGHT INTO WHAT WAS NECESSARY TO TURN THE COMPANY AROUND, MAKING IT MORE PROFITABLE AND INSPIRING PEOPLE TO PUT FORTH THEIR BEST EFFORTS. THE RESULTS SPEAK FOR THEMSELVES."

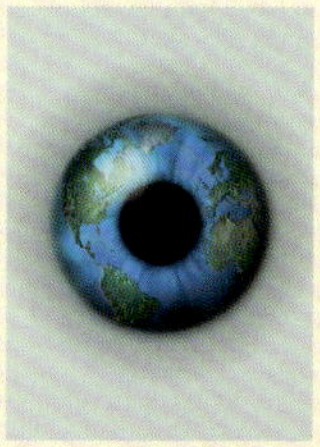

Creating a formidable R&D operation is one of the priorities of the New Allergan. This Irvine research facility will grow to house well over 1,000 people by 2004. To be added are a 57,000-square-foot pharmaceutical science building and a separate 15,000-square-foot building to house a new state-of-the-art research laboratory. The 1998 annual report cover featured the eye at left, symbolizing Allergan's worldwide prominence in eye-care products.

One of the things I wanted to set up here," says Pyott, "was a company that would act swiftly and decisively, re-creating a fast, small-company culture with a crystal-clear strategy." In the new millennium, Pyott predicts, "The fast and the focused will be the winners."

"David brings a strong marketing and consumer product background to the organization," says Boyer. "Yet he is very receptive to R&D. One of our concerns when we hired him was his minimal experience in the pharmaceutical industry, but he stepped in and was a very quick study on the subject. He understands the need for developing new products and improving our existing ones."

"His renewed focus on marketing is critical," says Gavin Herbert. "There are two key elements to building a pharmaceutical company. One is developing differentiated, patented new products, and the other is marketing. If you focus your energy on those two areas, everything else is going to fall into place."

New Strengths

Things are indeed falling into place. Already, superior G&A performance is being realized through the smaller, restructured corporate center, with specific G&A services under the direct control of their respective regions or business units. By streamlining G&A functions and increasing automation, Frank Tunney says, "We eliminate unnecessary labor and allow our associates to concentrate their time as knowledge workers, on thinking and strategizing rather than on administrative work."

The final phase of the plant consolidations that began in the early 1990s establishes a global network of four regional plants on the major continents, plus a global surgical plant in Puerto Rico. "A global network allows you to manage capacity on a worldwide basis," says Jackie Schiavo, "and that allows you to provide an effective, logistical response to markets and opportunities as they change." Trans-shipability between markets boosts responsiveness, and the smaller network of plants enables Allergan to better ensure global product line consistency. "Having one plant in each region is also quite important," Schiavo notes, "because we want to have regional flexibility to meet the strategic local market needs." Yet the network retains a single global operations management structure, so that everyone is working toward the same strategic and tactical goal.

Commercial operations have been decentralized into four regions: Irvine, California (North America); High Wycombe, England (Europe/Africa/Middle East); Sao Paulo, Brazil (Latin America); and Hong Kong (Asia Pacific). Previously, to Pyott's surprise, both Latin America and Asia Pacific were headquartered in Irvine. "Having worked in Asia Pacific," Pyott says, "I knew very keenly that if you're not there and you don't smell that tropical air in the morning, frankly, you don't know what's going on." Regional presidents and their staffs are now in closer contact with their customers and their cultures.

Early criticism of the New Allergan is giving way to praise as the focus shifts from trimming the fat to boosting the brains, most notably in research and development. R&D spending increased by about 40 percent in Pyott's first year alone. A $70 million expansion plan for the Irvine headquarters, announced in April 1999, earmarks the majority of the new space for R&D. The plan includes a 57,000-square-foot pharmaceutical sciences facility, slated to open in 2002. A separate 150,000-square-foot building, which will house a state-of-the-art research facility, is due for completion in 2004. By then, the R&D staff will have grown from approximately 800 to well over 1,000. "The biggest single employee pool will be scientists," a local newspaper quoted Pyott as saying. "It will be more of a research campus with me as a small tenant."

Against that backdrop, Pyott will lead Allergan into a new and decidedly different phase of its life. While the company remains committed to market leadership, innovation and growth in eye care and skin care, it is also expanding its scope as research and markets warrant.

"Our philosophy and our strategy," says Les Kaplan, "is to be a specialty pharmaceutical company, where the number of physicians in the field is small enough to permit Allergan to put together a sales force and market a product efficiently." Potential products for broader markets, which can't be adequately addressed with a small, focused sales force, may be licensed out to other companies. "The value from the molecule may be best realized by putting it into the hands of somebody who already has an existing sales structure and a name that is well recognized by doctors who would use the product," says George Lasezkay, corporate vice president, corporate development. "If we can cut the right deal, out-licensing can create significant value for our shareholders."

Allergan will develop more differentiated products from molecule to market than ever before. "We now have an R&D capability to generate our own new chemical entities, which is something that didn't exist before 1990. We relied on in-licensing totally," Gavin says. Allergan's current R&D capabilities expand the company's options. "In order to really make it into the big leagues, you have to have the capability to do your own synthesis," he continues. Allergan's R&D team couldn't agree more. "Allergan has come to appreciate that the only way we're going to grow is to develop novel products that meet unmet medical needs," says Larry Wheeler, vice president, biological science. The company's commitment to R&D gives its brilliant corps of scientists the freedom to "go where the science takes us, even into additional therapeutic areas," says John Gibson, senior vice president, pharmaceutical development.

Yet some degree of in-licensing, also known as "search and development," must continue. "We can't invent all of the innovative products we need to compete in the next century," says Lasezkay. "Search and development will be as important as research and development, and both have the same

Scientists like Michael Stern, above, will help Allergan generate its own chemical entities and take them from molecule to market. But there is still a willingness to in-license as well as out-license products other companies could market more effectively.

The Human Genome Project: Leveling the Playing Field

"There's a tremendous revolution in science going on right now," says Les Kaplan, "and it will level the playing field." Kaplan is referring to the Human Genome Project, an ongoing effort to sequence all 100,000 human genes and pinpoint which ones, or combinations of them, are responsible for various disease states.

"It's going to be an incredible tour de force," says Herbert Boyer, who is a founder of Genentech, Inc. "We have subsets of populations that respond differently to certain drugs. This may provide a way of formulating very sophisticated diagnoses and tailoring treatment to individuals."

"We're going to find out that what we thought was one disease is actually 20 diseases," predicts Mike Garst. "It's going to take a huge market and fragment it into many smaller segments. And each of those is probably going to have a distinct drug or drug class that works for it." Such fragmentation could benefit smaller companies like Allergan, which can't compete in billion-dollar markets.

"Anything less than $300 million in sales is too small for most big pharmaceutical companies to go after," David Pyott explains. "Whereas I say, give me a couple of hundred-million-dollar products. For a little company like ours, that has a huge effect."

Beyond mapping the genes, predicts Boyer, "What will be most valuable in the future of medicine is understanding how molecules interact with one another. There's such a delicate balance that even a single molecule can trigger a whole cascade of interactions that affect the course of a disease or the effectiveness of a drug."

goal: to bring innovative products to the market as fast as possible. The companies that can do that will be the ones that survive and flourish."

Some exciting new compounds are in the works at Allergan's laboratories in Irvine and around the world, and their reach could extend to millions of people worldwide. What will be the Ocuflox, the Acular and the Alphagan of the next 50 years? Here is a glimpse of the company's Stars of the Future.

Stars of the Future

Retinoids

There is a widespread and well-founded belief that Allergan's retinoid research could change the face of the company in the new millennium. Certainly it has become a top research commitment. "Allergan is in a leadership position here," says Les Kaplan. "We've made a strong investment in this area over a number of years, and I think we have some of the best scientists in the world working in this field."

Sixteen years after he first began researching retinoids in dermatology, Rosh Chandraratna and his colleagues are headed in more directions than they'd ever imagined. "Retinoids are definitely useful in dermatology," Chandraratna says, "but that is just the tip of the iceberg. Because of their fundamental mechanisms of action, we believe they're going to be useful in treating a heck of a lot of other diseases."

One new frontier is the treatment of diabetes. Compounds called RXR agonists appear to function as insulin sensitizers, addressing the fundamental problem of Type II diabetes. In 1998, Allergan teamed up with the Parke-Davis Pharmaceutical Research Division of the Warner-Lambert Company to develop and commercialize the two leading RXR compounds for the treatment of diabetes and other metabolic diseases. "We felt we didn't have the muscle or the size to develop or market a diabetes drug alone," Chandraratna says of the collaboration. "But if the first generation drugs work, from a scientific viewpoint it will be very satisfying, we will make money through the collaboration, and there will always be second generation drugs."

An entirely new class of retinoids called RAR antagonists works by blocking retinoid receptor function. Human clinical trials are studying the use of the RAR antagonist AGN-4310 for the treatment of psoriasis and eczema. Chandraratna believes the research in this area could spawn discoveries of therapeutic applications for many other diseases.

Botox

Botox, one of Allergan's leading players of the 1990s, is also one of its brightest stars of the future. At the dawn of the new millennium, Botox is already approved by the FDA for treating strabismus (crossed eyes) and blepharospasm (eyelid spasms), but its potential applications cover a variety of movement and neuromuscular disorders, many of which are large potential markets. "The areas Allergan is pursuing include cervical dystonia, spasticity in adults who have had strokes and juvenile cerebral palsy," says Les Kaplan. The company has registrations in select countries for those indications and Phase III clinical studies are under way in the U.S.

The American Academy of Otolaryngology, American Academy of Neurology and an advisory board of the National Institutes of Health have endorsed the use of Botox in the treatment of cervical dystonia. Botox is also in Phase III clinical trial for use in the prevention of hyperhydrosis, or excess sweating.

Roger Aoki, neurotoxin research team leader, has described Botox as "beautifully created by nature to be one of the most effective drug delivery systems ever designed." Once injected, Botox binds to specific receptors at the nerve endings, blocking the release of the neurotransmitter acetylcholine. Without acetylcholine, brain signals that tell the muscle to contract or spasm are blocked and the muscle becomes temporarily paralyzed. The effects of a single injection last for three to four months.

"One of the surprises of the off-label use of Botox for cosmetic treatment," notes Aoki, "is that patients are coming back to their doctors and saying, 'You know, I haven't had a migraine headache in a long time." Such serendipity has expanded Botox research into the areas of migraine headache, chronic tension headache and lower back pain, all large markets where current treatments are often inadequate. Phase III clinical studies are underway for all of these potential indications except tension headache, which is in Phase II study. If studies support its safety and efficacy, Botox could become the first prophylactic treatment for the prevention of migraine headaches.

"We have a marvelous opportunity to build on Botox," adds John Gibson. That doesn't just mean finding new applications for the toxin. Aoki's team is busy researching Botox's mechanism of action. "If we can identify and control the key steps, we can do our own protein engineering on the toxin, dialing in characteristics that would be better for one type of clinical use versus another." The result would be a selection of Botox products, tailored by duration and other features to various clinical applications. Even further on the horizon, but already promising in animal studies, is the possible use of Botox to stimulate nerve regeneration. If studies prove it to be safe and effective, Botox could become a truly revolutionary treatment for patients with spinal cord injuries. And the research doesn't stop with Botox. "We're looking at the whole family of neurotoxins and other types of toxins," says Aoki.

Hypotensive Lipids

One of Allergan's most promising opportunities in the near future is a product in development that would be used to lower intraocular pressure (IOP) in patients with glaucoma. The product, AGN 192024, is a hypotensive lipid, derived from prostaglandins.

Glaucoma affects some 67 million people worldwide and is a leading cause of blindness. In a healthy eye, fluid circulates through the opening of the pupil, passes into the space between the iris and the cornea and

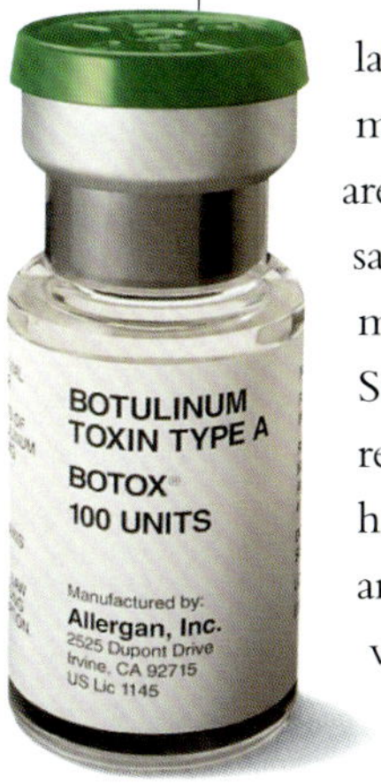

Botulinum toxin type A is superbly effective and safe when tiny amounts are injected into eye muscles. Allergan's Botox has been approved by regulatory agencies around the world for a variety of exciting uses.

drains out of the eye through a mesh of tissue called the drainage angle. In a patient with glaucoma, the passage of fluid through the drainage angle slows or stops, causing an increase in intraocular pressure. This rise in pressure injures the nerve fibers and blood vessels of the optic nerve, ultimately causing blindness.

"There's dramatic room for improvement in IOP-lowering agents," says Mike Garst, vice president, chemical science, "especially in the diminishing of side effects." Clinical studies to date indicate that AGN 192024 improves the flow of fluid out of the eye, thereby reducing IOP. Compared with Xalatan, the leading IOP-lowering agent and the most-prescribed ophthalmic pharmaceutical in the U.S., AGN 192024 has a superior safety profile in preclinical studies. Allergan plans to submit a New Drug Application in the U.S. in 2000 and an European Marketing Authorisation Application in Europe shortly thereafter. AGN 192024 would compete directly with Xalatan, which is expected to exceed $500 million in annual sales in 2000. "It could be revolutionary in terms of financial reward for this company," Gibson says.

AGN 192024 is significant to the company not only because of its potential, but also because it would be only the second product synthesized entirely in-house. (Tazorac was the first.) Its patent doesn't expire until 2014.

Neuroprotective Agents

For the last 150 years, the treatment of glaucoma has been limited to compounds that reduce intraocular pressure (IOP). Yet even when IOP is managed, glaucoma patients continue to lose vision over time. In some cases, the optic nerve is damaged even when IOP is normal. "There's something else going on with the optic nerve," says Larry Wheeler. "We're working on compounds that directly affect the optic nerve, and they may or may not lower pressure." One factor appears to be the release of excess glutamate in response to glaucomatous injury. The eye's retinal ganglion cells normally process visual information and transmit it to the brain, but glutamate activates receptors in the cells that cause them to die.

Allergan is investigating agents that may prevent or reduce vision loss by protecting the retinal ganglion cells. Allergan's focus, says Les Kaplan, is on "survival factors that can possibly keep those cells alive, even when they are getting signals to die off." It's called neuroprotection.

Topping the list of potential neuroprotective agents is Alphagan (brimonidine), the company's newest IOP-lowering drug. "We have good evidence in the laboratory that Alphagan is neuroprotective," Wheeler says. "We've discovered by serendipity that there is a protective process in the retina when you activate an alpha$_2$ receptor." Proving it in humans won't be easy, however. Researchers are completing human proof-of-principle studies to demonstrate that Alphagan protects retinal ganglion cells. Even if brimonidine itself proves not to be the optimal molecule for neuroprotection, Allergan is heading in the right direction. "I think of Alphagan as the bridge to the future," Larry Wheeler says.

Also under investigation for neuroprotection is a glutamate NMDA receptor agonist called memantine, which has been shown to protect the retinal ganglion cells in primates. A four-year, multi-center study of 1,000 patients will document the effects of memantine in humans.

"Up until now, there have been no direct sight-preserving agents," notes John Gibson. "It would be absolutely phenomenal if we could truly reduce blindness with brimonidine or memantine."

Retinal Disease Project

Allergan's retinal disease project is investigating possible treatments for age-related macular degeneration (ARMD), a leading cause of blindness that affects some 13 million people worldwide. As its name suggests, ARMD is a disease of aging in which new blood vessels grow between the layers of the retina in a process called angiogenesis. Edema, or swelling, from these leaky new vessels causes the layers of the retina to split and vision to be lost. ARMD occurs to some degree in everyone, but patients who lose their central vision suffer the most, losing the ability to read, watch television or drive. As the population ages, the incidence of ARMD is rising dramatically.

"ARMD is the only ocular disease for which there's no effective treatment," Garst says. A form of laser treatment called photo dynamic therapy offers some promise, but it would need to be repeated every three to four months and accompanied with drug therapy.

The National Eye Institute and American Academy of Ophthalmology have named macular degeneration their #1 disease target. "Macular degeneration is the most important area to concentrate on now and for the future," says Stephen Ryan, dean of medicine, University of Southern California Medical School and president, Doheny Eye

Institute. "Allergan is making an investment in the field, and I think that shows Allergan is appropriately anticipating the future."

"The direction Allergan is going is to try to find a drug that prevents angiogenesis to begin with," says Garst. Since angiogenesis is also a key area of cancer research, Allergan initiated a collaboration with Sugen, Inc., a company that specializes in cancer research, to leverage their expertise and experience in blocking new blood vessel formation. "I won't say this is the last frontier in ophthalmology," Garst says, "but it's the next frontier. It's a bigger market than glaucoma."

Cyclosporine

On another pioneering frontier, Allergan is literally on the brink of revolutionizing the treatment of dry eye, a troublesome condition that affects about 3.6 percent of the population. Previously, dry eye has been managed with artificial tear products that act as "palliatives," says Research Investigator Mike Stern. "All they do is lubricate the ocular surface, so you get very temporary, almost momentary relief, and then it disappears."

Over the course of more than a decade, Stern and his colleagues have investigated the cause and treatment of dry eye, which at its worst is virtually debilitating. "We discovered that these people are suffering from an immune-based inflammation of the ocular surface." His group has demonstrated that cyclosporine interrupts the inflammatory process that causes dry eye. Their findings led to the development of Restasis. With U.S. and select international launches anticipated in 2000, Restasis would be the first therapeutic in a market estimated to be well in excess of $100 million worldwide.

"We should own this market," Stern says. "Restasis will place Allergan as a company that's stepping into a leadership role, and I think that just reaps all sorts of benefits for the company, even outside the market for dry eye."

Next on the agenda for Stern's group: attacking the disease earlier, either with the next generation cyclosporine product, or with another potential product, Androgen Tears. Dry eye is most common in pre-menopausal and pregnant women — populations with reduced levels of circulating androgens. "When the androgen level drops below a critical threshold," Stern says, "the anti-inflammatory environment is compromised, potentially leading to dry eye."

Ophthalmic Surgical Products

Allergan's multifocal Array is first in a new generation of IOLs and sets the standard for the new millennium. No IOL has come closer to the ultimate goal of restoring natural visual accommodation.

"When we talk about best outcomes for the patient," says Dan McWard, vice president, global surgical business, "the Array is head and shoulders above anything that's in the market today. This unique, patented technology provides a senior patient the type of vision that they haven't had for probably 20 or 30 years, or in some cases never."

"The future may be in restoring more natural accommodation and expansion of these technologies to the treatment of other refractive errors — sort of the marrying of refractive surgery and cataract surgery together," says Patricia Knight, vice president of research and development. A phacic IOL might be developed for patients with presbyopia, the vision problem that occurs naturally with aging. Already, some doctors will replace both lenses in presbyopic patients who have cataracts in just one eye. "I think many ophthalmologists are approaching their cataract patients like refractive surgery patients," Knight says. "They want to leave them spectacle-free as much as possible."

Expanding the Five Business Areas

The Stars of the Future hold great promise for Allergan's long-term success. But for the immediate future, Allergan is banking its success on existing products in its five primary business areas: ophthalmic pharmaceuticals or "eye Rx"; neuromuscular; ophthalmic surgery; contact-lens-care products; and skin care.

Ophthalmic Pharmaceuticals

Allergan enters the new millennium as a world leader in eye Rx. "I can say with a lot of pride that worldwide we have the largest ophthalmic pharmaceutical sales force, even larger than Merck," Pyott says. "I think that paints what vision we have for the future." The enthusiastic and expanding base of Alphagan customers helps Allergan's position by creating what Pyott describes as a "halo effect." "When you're at the top of their mind through Alphagan, our star product, many ophthalmologists just keep prescribing other products from the same company."

"When you have an innovative product," says Mike Ball, who heads the global eye Rx business, "your other products tend to follow along. It keeps the company image out there." Ball predicts there will be a sizable worldwide market for Restasis, the first prescription treatment for dry eye. "This looks

Allergan Foundation

Allergan established the Allergan Foundation in 1998 to increase the company's involvement in the communities in which its employees live and work. Education in math and science is its top priority, followed by health care, civic programs and the arts. Tom Burnham, vice president of human resources, is president of the Allergan Foundation. ("This is my Saturday morning job," he says.) In its first year, the foundation made grants to the University of California at Irvine, local school districts' math and science programs, United Cerebral Palsy, Helen Keller International, Hoag Memorial Hospital, American Red Cross and Irvine Children's Fund. Currently working with approximately $20 million, the foundation plans grants of some million dollars a year.

THE ALLERGAN FOUNDATION

to be a very dissatisfied marketplace that we hope to satisfy quite nicely." While marketing will initially target physicians, "further down the road, this product may be a good candidate for direct-to-consumer advertising because it's a chronic issue and patients may have given up hope of ever finding anything."

Ball predicts Acular, Ocuflox and Alphagan will all survive well into the new millennium. "Even when their patents run out, they will still have staying power," he says. With no new generic competition expected before 2003, Allergan has time to prepare. "By that time, some of the new products in the pipeline will be well on their way."

Ball expresses confidence in Allergan's ability to "get the most out of our molecules" by remaining results-oriented and taking an aggressive approach to managing the life-cycles of products. "We need to ensure that we make the most of our discoveries in R&D. A molecule is a terrible thing to waste."

Neuromuscular

Botox has been growing at a rate of about 40 percent a year and achieved 1998 sales in excess of $100 million in the U.S. alone. It now faces its first neurotoxin competition in the U.S. from a botulinum toxin type B product marketed by Athena. Still, the rate of Botox's growth is so rapid and the promise of expanded indications so great, that while competition will have some impact, abundant opportunities for continued growth will still exist.

Les Kaplan predicts that Botox's future will be both in specialty fields, where Allergan markets the products, and in general fields, where Allergan may co-promote potential products to another firm. In calling this segment of the business "Neuromuscular," Allergan also leaves open the door to new compounds, such as other neurotoxins, and new indications, such as spinal cord injuries and pain.

Ophthalmic Surgical

Allergan holds the number one position in the foldable IOL market in Europe and number two worldwide. To become the leader, says Dan McWard, "We'll need to continue delivering new technologies that provide best uncorrected outcomes for patients." The Array, as the first-ever multifocal IOL, is clearly a step in that direction.

Having recently added the Sensar, an acrylic foldable IOL, to the product line, "We really have the widest offering of high technology small-incision lenses of anyone in the market," McWard says.

The company is also striving to become the #1 phacoemulsification company worldwide. Allergan released its new flagship phaco system, the Sovereign, in May 1999. "This is a quantum leap in phaco technology," McWard says. "We feel that the superior

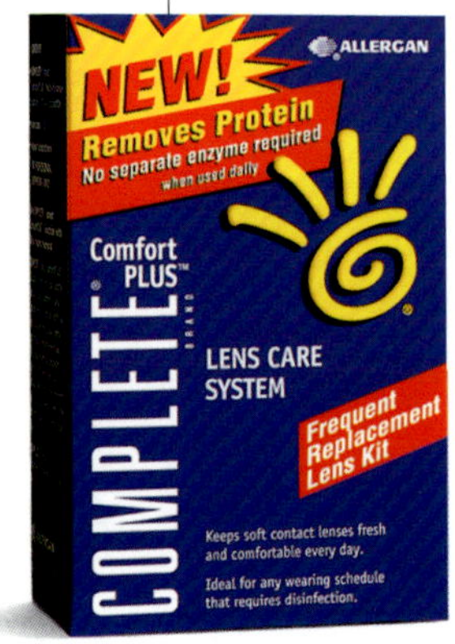

Complete Comfort Plus is an upgrade of Complete, introduced in 1994. This all-in-one-bottle liquid for contact lens care has helped propel Allergan into a #1 market position in Europe and #2 worldwide for lens care systems.

technology of the Sovereign, the improved fluidics, the computer-driven capabilities of the machine, will give it tremendous leg up on anybody else out there."

Being a full-service ophthalmic surgery company will continue to be a priority for Allergan in the future. Partnerships, such as that formed with Allegiance in the late 1990s in the U.S., will help the company continue to provide surgical kits, viscoelastics, and other supplies. "We feel that partnerships will help us propel our business and become more of a leader in this industry," McWard says.

Contact-Lens-Care Products

The contact lens care business is #2 worldwide, with market leadership in Europe and Japan. Jim Mazzo, leader of global lens-care products, says global market leadership is an attainable goal in the new millennium. "Our plans to allow us to continue our growth and attain the #1 position are tied directly to our strategic plan," Mazzo says. "That plan states that we will manage this business as a consumer business with a professional orientation. In addition, we will reinvest in consumer marketing and rapidly grow Complete, our one-bottle franchise, which is where the most market growth is occurring." Cost of goods reductions and marketing efficiencies will be captured and redirected toward our customers.

Skin Care

"The excitement in skin care is not in yesterday or today," says Mike Ball, president, North American region. "It's in the future." Allergan's leading skin-care products — Azelex for acne, Tazorac for psoriasis and acne, and the MD Forte line of alpha-hydroxy

Patents: The Lifeline to the Future

The life of a pharmaceutical company is largely dependent upon the strength and breadth of its patents. When patents expire, generics frequently erode the market share of successful pharmaceutical products. One reason investors are bullish about Allergan's future is its powerful patent portfolio.

An independent study published in 1998 described Allergan as a pharmaceutical industry "pioneer," based on the company's patents, "There's our future," Frank Tunney says, pointing to a copy of the study, "Patents."

While Allergan ranked 29th with regard to the total number of U.S. patents for new chemical entities (NCEs) in the study period of 1993–1997, the company was tops in patent references. Of Allergan's 975 citations in that time period, 925 were self-citations. "This suggests," the study said, "that Allergan has found a niche area that it is patenting around (and citing) very heavily, but that has been largely ignored by other companies." Or, as Tunney describes it, "The more self-citations, the more you're building a real intellectual property fortress."

The fortress is well-protected into the early years of the new millennium. "The good news is we don't have any products facing generic competition until 2003," Pyott notes. "While patent-life extension programs in R&D may not be the sexiest of items, they're now receiving very high attention."

acid products for photo damage — were growing by more than 30 percent a year in the late 1990s. But Allergan's future in skin care will be shaped mostly by new products and new formulations of Tazorac.

Tazorac is now expanding into the $600 million acne market with a topical formulation that will compete directly with other retinoid products like Retin A, many of which are $100 million products. Studies suggest that Tazorac applied to the face has advantages in some cases over currently available products.

An oral formulation in development would compete directly with the blockbuster acne drug, Accutane. "Even if we get just 10 percent of the oral market, it would be exceptionally exciting to our skin-care business," Ball says. "But if we get 30 percent or more, then you could be talking about something that completely changes Allergan as a company."

"I'm not at all concerned about generics," he adds, "because our patent life for Tazorac is through the year 2011." By then, new generation products will likely eclipse generic competition.

For now, Allergan's skin care efforts are focused on the U.S., where the sales and marketing infrastructure is established. Tazorac is sold overseas as Zorac through partners with greater inroads in the target markets.

The Global Future

Allergan begins the millennium with a strong presence on all four major continents and more than half of net sales coming from outside the United States. "Geographically the company has a rosy future," says board member Handel Evans. Indeed, the company is well-positioned to capitalize on opportunities for growth in key markets around the globe.

Asia Pacific

When David Pyott joined Allergan, his first international visit was to Japan, perhaps exemplifying the value he places on the company's future there. He and Schalon Newton, then-president of Allergan KK, Allergan's Japanese subsidiary, ceremonially received identical Japanese daruma dolls. Coloring one eye of the doll symbolizes a goal. "We colored in the eye to reach $200 million in sales," Newton says. "He brought his back to California. It's up in his office. I kept mine in my office, and basically that daruma sits there with its one eye looking at you, reminding you of this goal. And when you achieve it, you get to color in the other eye." Newton has since turned his daruma doll over to Masatake Akedo, who succeeds him as head of the Japanese business.

At the new millennium, Japan accounts for about 8 percent of Allergan's worldwide sales, most of it in surgical products. Akedo predicts the business will grow by 15 to 20 percent in the first five years of the millennium. "The idea of explosive growth in any other part of the world might depend upon a major acquisition," Akedo says, "but in Japan, where we haven't yet entered the eye-care pharmaceutical market, and we're at the very beginning of Botox, we now have the opportunity."

"We haven't been in the prescription business in Japan except to out-license our products because of some historical reasons relating to our joint venture with Santen there," says Dave Fellows, president, Asia Pacific region. In addition, Japan has been one of the most stringent regulatory environments in the world. But with the rules on drug clearance easing and costs of entering the market diminishing, a direct strategy is not a long way off. "The size of the sales force now doesn't have to be as big as it once did, so we believe Allergan will be able to have a direct entry into the pharmaceutical business in the first part of the new millennium," adds Fellows.

"Allergan's technologies will create a new paradigm in both the $1.2 billion prescription pharmaceutical market and the $450 million over-the-counter eye drop market," says Akedo. "Most Japanese eyedrop products are technologically virtually identical. Allergan's superior products will have a revolutionary impact in the OTC category."

Throughout the Asia Pacific region, the market for pharmaceutical products is largely

Asia Pacific offers an almost untapped market for Allergan. Consept F, a soft-lens disinfectant, has enjoyed a 33 percent increase in sales.

untapped. "Our pharmaceutical products are 15 or 16 percent of sales," Fellows says. "So we're relatively underdeveloped on the Rx side. In a sense, we're out of sync with the rest of the corporation because we don't have that huge platform to build on. Until we get into Korea in a big way and Japan in a big way, we're probably going to remain relatively underdeveloped in our Rx business."

Allergan's manufacturing facility in Hangzhou, China will help the Rx business develop and give the company a competitive advantage over U.S. competitors. Built in the late 1990s, the plant is a key component of Allergan's strategy to deliver products inexpensively throughout the region. While all Allergan plants are built to first-world standards, the China plant (like the one in Brazil) currently operates at slightly lower World Health Organization standards "because that's appropriate for that marketplace," says Jackie Schiavo, head of worldwide operations. "It will not be too long before everything will standardize at the higher level because these developing markets are raising their standards very quickly. Also, we want to use our global manufacturing strength, so we'll want to start exporting from those plants to first-world markets."

China's population of 1.2 billion could benefit significantly from the company's products, but the masses are difficult to reach. "It will be at least five to ten years before China emerges as a major ophthalmic market," Fellows predicts. "Worldwide, glaucoma is the largest segment, but in China, the glaucoma segment is tiny. In many cases, they don't go to see the opthalmologist until they're functionally blind. And at that point, drops aren't much help."

Allergan became the #1 ophthalmic company in India after just three years in the market, with sales exceeding $10 million by 1999. The Indian market for potential new products is vast and growing. The incidence of blindness there is 15 times that in the United States. The World Bank initiated a $150 million project to reduce blindness in India by setting up new clinics and hospitals. The project could increase awareness of ophthalmic problems among the Indian population, thereby significantly expanding the market.

Europe/Africa/Middle East

"Our region is similar to others," says Jim Mazzo, president, Europe/Africa/Middle East, "in that there are pressures on governments to reduce healthcare costs as the aging population continues to demand better, higher-quality and higher-cost services." Allergan is responding "by being proactive and understanding these issues, working with the governments and providing resources and data to support the introduction and acceptance of our products."

Europe is a collection of key markets for Allergan products. It is not yet a single market and may never truly be one, but it is moving in that direction. A single drug clearance agency approves pharmaceuticals for all of the European Union (EU), but individual countries still require separate procedures as well. Similarly, the CE Mark for medical devices indicates overall approval in the EU and is vital to a device's success in the region. The establishment of the Euro, a standard currency throughout Europe, is likely to stabilize prices between countries, helping Allergan ensure the profitability of its products.

Regulatory approvals are likely to become somewhat easier in Europe as the millennium progresses. Harmonization between the regulatory agencies of Europe, the U.S. and Japan would reduce the need for separate, costly and time-consuming clinical trials. Ideally, a single set of basic rules will be applied to clinical testing, which will significantly speed up the process.

Leandro Herrero, vice president, R&D Europe, says even as regulatory processes are standardized, the complexity and diversity of the region remains. In recognition of the region's diversity, Allergan is organized in Europe by language groups to facilitate communication and cultural understanding. "How people are treated for medical issues in Spain, my home country, and how they are treated in the U.K. are completely different. The technology is the same, the drugs are very similar, but the attitudes are different and the medical models are different. So embracing the diversity from any viewpoint — commercial, developmental, organizational — would be a criterion for success."

Latin America

Allergan's Latin American presence received a boost in the late 1990s with the establishment of regional headquarters in Sao Paulo and the appointment of Nelson Marques, a native of Brazil, as president. "The future looks bright for this region," Marques says. "It's one of the few regions in the world where there is still a lot of room for growth."

While Brazil is already a significant market for Allergan, Marques says the company has yet to realize its potential in Latin America's other key markets, Argentina and Mexico. "In Mexico, we have wonderful opportunities, either through new products or through acquisitions."

美國眼力健
世界護眼權威
COMPLETE

In several Southeast Asian markets, Allergan works with full-service distributors who provide sales, customer service, order fulfillment and other services. India, right, presents a vast and fast-growing marketing opportunity for Allergan — it is a nation in which almost 20 million people suffer from cataracts, and the incidence of blindness there is 15 times that in the United States. Allergan's joint venture with Nicholas Piramal is the #1 ophthalmic company in India.

The major concern in Latin America is the volatility of the macroeconomic situation. "Stability is a strange word for Latin America," Marques says, "but over the last few years the three primary markets have been pretty stable. I expect this to continue." He adds that economic alliances, such as NAFTA, will continue to shape the way Latin American countries do business in the new millennium.

North America

Despite Allergan's strong domestic position, there is plenty of room for growth. Key markets for existing products are expanding, particularly as the population ages, and even in areas of market leadership, there is always the opportunity to increase market share. On top of all of this, Mike Ball, regional president, sees a promising outflow of new products from R&D. "It's probably not right to call it an embarrassment of riches," he says, "but we've got a very interesting pipeline going forward."

Managed Care Organizations (MCOs) will continue to dictate the way the company sells products domestically for the foreseeable future. Formularies can already make or break a pharmaceutical product. In years to come, doctors may enter prescriptions into computers that immediately indicate whether or not a drug is on the payor's formulary. If it isn't, the doctor may be deterred from prescribing the drug to other patients, even if they are covered under a different plan. Formularies also give MCO's bargaining power over prices.

In late 1999, President Clinton proposed adding prescription drug coverage to Medicare for a small monthly premium.

Such a plan, if passed, could result in price controls that would harm pharmaceutical innovation.

The cost-conscious nature of healthcare in the new millennium requires a new approach to selling. "One of the ways we're trying to sell," Ball says, "is on the basis of bringing innovative products to physicians, not 'me-too' products. As we see more managed care coming along and more pharmacoeconomics being required, more innovation is necessary." To ensure the success of innovative products, "We'll be working as more of a business team with our partners, which will include managed care, Medicare, Medicaid and the providers.

"We have common interests in making sure the entire eye-care profession is moving forward." The company is increasingly using direct-to-consumer advertising to help bring patients into the doctor's office, where, if the ads are effective, they inquire about Allergan's products. "We have the capability of helping to shape the future of eye care in America," Ball says, "to the betterment of patients, physicians and the company."

The Allergan of the Future

With mergers and acquisitions now an overriding theme in the pharmaceutical industry, it is logical to wonder what Allergan might look like as the new millennium progresses. "I think companies use this strategy of consolidation often for the wrong reasons — usually because their pipeline was too dry," says David Pyott. "There might be some synergies; there might be some cost-cutting, but that's just a short-term fix."

For now, Allergan remains an intact, highly specialized pharmaceutical company, with partnerships, alliances, in-licensing and out-licensing to balance its strengths and weaknesses. "Partnerships among companies — both big and small, and of equal sizes — is the wave of the future for the pharmaceutical industry," George Lasezkay says. "Some of the things we'll be doing in coming years will be surprising, a little unconventional, but ultimately they will create lots of shareholder value and be to our long-range benefit."

Partnerships also help keep Allergan lean. "The big research-based pharmaceutical companies are like super tankers," says board member Henry Wendt. "They carry a lot, have a lot of momentum, but they're not agile."

"Maybe five years down the road, I see the big companies breaking up again into smaller, more focused parts," Pyott says. "I think these lumbering giants are going to pay the price if they continue to lumber."

"Our tasks are to produce new innovative products, sell them aggressively, and show sustainable growth year over year in terms of sales and earnings," Lasezkay says. "Success and innovation will invariably make us an interesting company, but in any event, top-notch performance is our target."

While corporate growth is hard to predict, Gavin Herbert says the company should set lofty goals. "It's important to have growth targets that cause people to stretch their imaginations," Herbert says. "A $4 billion goal for the year 2010 is an achievable objective."

"Speaking from the board, we expect success in the future," Herbert Boyer says. "We're delighted with management, but we'll always provide our best recommendations and guidance. We'll always question, always look for a better strategy, always seek better performance. And we trust that they'll deliver."

"The prospects for Allergan have never been brighter," says Frank Tunney, who has been with the company since 1986. "We've got great people, products and market positions; a strong R&D pipeline; excellent leadership — all of the ingredients for success."

"Allergan has been an enormous part of my life for half a century," says Gavin Herbert. "Now the company is in other hands, and they are strong and capable hands. Allergan's leaders have charted a promising future for the company, and I wish them Godspeed."

As Allergan approaches the millennium, its prospects for the future have never been brighter. Led by David Pyott, left, and Herb Boyer, right, the company has refocused its energies on core businesses of specialty eye care and neurotoxins (in which it enjoys #2 and #1 positions, respectively worldwide) and has an R&D pipeline full of innovative formulations that will spur future prosperity.

BOARD OF DIRECTORS OF ALLERGAN, INC. (as of November 1, 1999)

Back row, from left: Lester J. Kaplan, Michael R. Gallagher, Leonard D. Schaeffer, Henry Wendt. Middle row, from left: Handel E. Evans, William R. Grant, Gavin S. Herbert, Herbert W. Boyer, Ronald M. Cresswell. Front row, from left: Louis T. Rosso, David E. I. Pyott, Karen R. Osar.

CURRENT BOARD MEMBERS

Herbert W. Boyer, Ph.D.
Chairman, Allergan, Inc.

Ronald M. Cresswell, Ph.D.
Retired Chairman, Parke-Davis Pharmaceutical Research

Handel E. Evans
Independent Consultant

Michael R. Gallagher
Chief Executive Officer, Playtex Products, Inc.

William R. Grant
Chairman, Galen Associates

Gavin S. Herbert
Chairman Emeritus, Allergan, Inc.

Lester J. Kaplan, Ph.D.
Corporate Vice President, Science & Technology

Karen R. Osar
Senior Vice President and Chief Financial Officer, Westvaco Corporation

David E. I. Pyott
President and Chief Executive Officer, Allergan, Inc.

Louis T. Rosso
Chairman Emeritus, Beckman Coulter, Inc.

Leonard D. Schaeffer
Chairman and Chief Executive Officer, WellPoint Health Networks, Inc.

Henry Wendt
Chairman, Global Health Care Partners

FORMER BOARD MEMBERS

1970s

Gavin S. Herbert Sr.
Chairman, Allergan Pharmaceuticals

John A. Biles, Ph.D
Dean, School of Pharmacy, University of Southern California

Hazen A. Boucher Jr.
Vice President, Consyne Corporation

Earl Clark
Vice Chairman, Transamerica Corporation

Lloyd E. Cotsen
Chief Executive Officer, Neutrogena, Inc.

Robert A. Hardt
Pharmaceutical Consultant

Richard P. Hausman
Executive Vice President, Allergan Pharmaceuticals

C. B. William Howell
Retired President, Geigy Pharmaceutical Division of CIBA-Corporation

Irving H. Leopold, M.D.
Senior Vice President, Medical Affairs, Allergan Pharmaceuticals

William S. Little
Retired Executive Vice President, Becton, Dickinson and Company

Keith C. Lumpkin
Senior Vice President and Treasurer, Allergan Pharmaceuticals

John G. Monkman
President of L.A.D. Drug Company

Thomas E. O'Sullivan
Attorney at Law

John B. Parker
President, Parker Properties

Jon C. Thorson, M.D.
Chairman, Optical Sciences Group, Inc.

Harold L. Upjohn, M.D.
Vice President, Research and Development, Allergan Pharmaceuticals

Gavin S. Younkin
Retired Vice President of Honeywell, Inc.

1980s and 1990s

David B. Bruns
Corporate Vice President and President, Europe Region, Allergan, Inc.

Tamara J. Erickson
Senior Vice President and Managing Director, Arthur D. Little, Inc.

Richard J. Flamson III
Chairman, Security Pacific Corporation

Howard E. Greene Jr.
Chairman and Chief Executive Officer, Amylin Pharmaceuticals, Inc.

Harry Groome III
Chairman, Consumer Healthcare, SmithKline Beecham, p.l.c.

Richard M. Haugen
Executive Vice President and Chief Operating Officer, Allergan, Inc.

Kenneth N. Kermes
Group Corporate Development Director, SmithKline Beecham, p.l.c.

Leslie G. McCraw
Chairman and Chief Executive Officer, Fluor Corporation

William C. Shepherd
Chairman, President and Chief Executive, Allergan, Inc.

EXECUTIVE COMMITTEE OF ALLERGAN, INC. (as of November 1, 1999)

Back row, from left: James V. Mazzo, Corporate Vice President and President, Europe/Africa/Middle East Region and Global Lens Care Products; David A. Fellows, Corporate Vice President and President, Asia Pacific Region; Francis R. Tunney, Jr., Corporate Vice President — Administration, General Counsel and Secretary; George M. Lasezkay, Corporate Vice President, Corporate Development. Middle row, from left: Nelson R. A. Marques, Corporate Vice President and President, Latin America Region; Lester J. Kaplan, Corporate Vice president and President, Research & Development and Global Botox; F. Michael Ball, Corporate Vice Presdient and President, North America Region and Global Eye Rx Business; Eric Brandt, Corporate Vice President and Chief Financial Officer. Front row, from left: David E. I. Pyott, Allergan President and Chief Executive Officer; and Jacqueline Schiavo, Corporate Vice President, Worldwide Operations.

ALLERGAN EXECUTIVE COMMITTEE

F. Michael Ball
Corporate Vice President and President, North America Region

Eric K. Brandt
Corporate Vice President and Chief Financial Officer

David A. Fellows
Corporate Vice President and President, Asia Pacific Region

Lester J. Kaplan, Ph.D.
Corporate Vice President, Science and Technology

George M. Lasezkay
Corporate Vice President, Corporate Development

Nelson R. A. Marques
Corporate Vice President and President, Latin America Region

James V. Mazzo
Corporate Vice President and President, Europe Region

David E. I. Pyott
President and Chief Executive Officer

Jacqueline Schiavo
Corporate Vice President, Worldwide Operations

Francis R. Tunney Jr.
Corporate Vice President, Administration-General Counsel and Secretary

Allergan Milestone Timeline

1950
January 27th, company is founded and incorporated in Los Angeles, California, by Gavin S. Herbert Sr.

Gavin Herbert Jr. and Sr. begin compounding ophthalmic products for physicians according to new FDA sterility rules. Soon add nasal products, one of which contains neoantergan, an antihistamine. An ophthalmologist working with the Herberts suggests using it as an anti-allergy eye drop to treat allergic conjunctivitis. The product, called Allergan, gave birth to the company's name.

1953
Allergan develops *Cortefrin*, the first cortisone eye drop to treat inflammation of the eye.

1957
Gavin Herbert Jr. moves the company to the Halliburton Building in downtown Los Angeles, California.

1958
First product, *Prednefrin*, launched nationally.

1960
Sales reach $.5 million.

1962
$1.0 million in sales.

Company moves to Santa Ana, in Orange County, California (30,000 sq.ft.).

1964
Establishes marketing subsidiary in Canada.

1966
William C. Shepherd joins Allergan as a formulation chemist.

1967
The first Allergan national sales meeting is held in Santa Ana, California.

1968
Establishes marketing subsidiary in Australia.

Purchases Irvine property — 24 acres.

Erects Von Karman building (60,000 sq. ft.).

1969
G.S. Herbert Laboratories is founded.

1970
First international manufacturing and distribution facility opens in Mexico City.

Sales reach $10.0 million (300 employees).

First public stock offering of 280,000 shares at $15.00 per share.

1971
Company moves to Irvine headquarters.

Opens manufacturing facility in Puerto Rico.

1975
Introduces first enzymatic soft lens cleaner tablet named *Soflens*.

1977
Gavin S. Herbert Sr. dies on January 12.

Listed on NYSE (for the first time).

1978
Opens manufacturing facility in Westport, Ireland.

1980
Sales hit $100 million.

SmithKline merger (Price: $260 million).

1984
Retnoid research begins.

William C. Shepherd is named president of Allergan.

1986
American Medical Optics acquisition is complete. (Price: $165 million.) AMO is a manufacturer of surgical products and IOL's.

Allergan Pharmaceuticals, Inc., is renamed as Allergan, Inc.

1987
Sales hit $500 million.

International Hydron acquisition, a manufacturer of contact lenses. (Price: $155 million)

1989
Company spun out by SmithKline. Listed on NYSE (for the second time).

1991
Oculinum, Inc., acquisition, creators of Botox product; company thus enters the neural care market.

Sells Humphrey Instruments to Carl Zeiss Co.

Schering AG licenses Azelex to Allergan (azelaic acid for treatment of mild to moderate acne). Approved for marketing in the U.S. in September of 1995.

1992
William C. Shepherd is named chief executive officer of Allergan, Inc.

Ligand joint venture is formed.

LOA Argentina acquisition (manufactures and sells ophthalmic medications).

Sells Americas contact lens business to Ocular Sciences.

Gensia agreement: *adenosine* regulating agent for the eye disease.

1993
Shareholder lawsuit dismissed.

Sells International contact lens business to Hydron, U.K.

Sandoz agreement: *Cyclosporine A* for serious dry eye.

Schein Pharmaceutical distribution agreement to market generic versions of some Allergan products currently off-patent in the U.S. Thus far, generic versions exist of *Betagan* (3/94) and *Propine* (6/94).

1994

Gavin S. Herbert retires from active management, but continues as chairman of the board.

New $40 million R&D facility opens. Campus totals 650,000 sq. ft. with master plan rights to a total of 925,000 sq. ft.

IOPTEX acquisition (IOL's) finalized.

Piramal joint venture. Company to manufacture and market Allergan eye care products in India.

Ioptex acquisition of IOL's.

1995

Optical Micro Systems acquisition.

Laboratorios Frumtost SA Industrias Farmaceuticas acquisition by Allergan-LOK Productos Farmaceutcos, LTDA. Ophthalmic and ear-nose-throat medications.

Herald Pharmacal acquisition, a leader in the aesthetic skin care market.

Gavin S. Herbert retires as chairman of the board and becomes chairman emeritus.

Sales hit $1 billion.

Allergan Ligand Retnoid Therapeutics, Inc., (ALRT) formed to replace the joint venture from 7/92. This newly public company will accelerate the research, development and commercialization efforts of the synthetic retnoids which were originally part of the joint venture.

Peptech (U.K.) agreement for development and commercialization of oral drug for severe psoriasis.

Santen-Allergan purchase of 50% balance of shares of Japanese joint venture (lens care).

Formosa Optical (Taiwan) agreement to promote Allergan lens care products in Taiwan and China.

Lens care business from Pilkington Barnes Hind, a strategic geographic acquisition based primarily in Japan. This doubles Allergan's lens care business in the market.

1996

Strategic restructuring of worldwide organization.

SUGEN collaboration to identify, develop and commercialize novel compounds utilizing SUGENs proprietary small molecule signal transduction inhibition technology for ophthalmic applications. Promising for age-related macular degeneration and diabetic retinopathy.

Cambridge Neuroscience (CNS) collaboration for the treatment of glaucoma with a potential vision sparing drug. Brings together CNSs nerve protection expertise and ion channel blocking molecules with AGNs research, development and commercialization expertise.

William C. Shepherd becomes chairman of the board.

1997

William C. Shepherd steps down as CEO, chairman and president of Allergan, Inc.

Allergan and Ligand split the rights to ALRT and each company received exclusive rights to the ALRT technology.

1998

David E.I. Pyott appointed president and CEO of Allergan, Inc.

Dr. Herbert W. Boyer becomes Allergan's new chairman of the board.

The Allergan Foundation is established for the purpose of donating money to different charity organizations such as education and health care throughout the community.

President David Pyott restructures Allergan and nicknames it the "New Allergan."

Allergan enters a multi-year research collaboration with the Parke-Davis Pharmaceutical Research Division of the Warner-Lambert Company to identify, develop and commercialize treatment for metabolic diseases.

China manufacturing plant opens in Hangzhou.

1999

David Pyott joins the board of Pharmaceutical Research and Manufacturers of America (PhRMA).

Allergan, Inc.'s business model becomes a part of a permanent research collection at the Smithsonian's National Museum of American History.

Allergan and ACADIA Pharmaceuticals enter into a license and research collaboration agreement to discover, develop and commercialize compounds for glaucoma.

Allergan enters a multi-year agreement with 3M Pharmaceuticals to co-promote Allergan's product *Tazorac* in the U.S. market.

Allergan forms a long-term marketing, sales and development partnership with Pierre Fabre Dermatologie for commercializing Zorac in continental Europe and surrounding territories.

2000

On January 27th, Allergan celebrates its first 50 years. Today it is as a technology driven, global health care company providing eye care and specialty pharmaceutical products. As a leader in the development and commercialization of products in the eye care, pharmaceutical, ophthalmic surgical device, over-the-counter contact lens care, movement disorder and dermatological markets, Allergan delivers value to its customers by satisfying unmet medical needs and improving patients' lives around the world.

GLOSSARY

A

Acular – A topical nonsteriodal anti-inflammatory drug (NSAID) intended for ophthalmic use.

Age-Related Macular Degeneration (ARMD) – Degeneration of the macular area of the retina of the eye, characterized by the loss of central vision and acuity.

AHA (Alpha Hydroxy Acids) Products – A compound found in Allergan skin care products.

Azelex – An acne therapy that refines and improves skin's texture and overall appearance.

Allergan Eye Drops – One of Allergan's first products, used for treatment of allergies.

Allergan Nasal Drops – One of Allergan's first products, also used for treating allergies.

Alphagan – A selective alpha agonist that lowers the high intraocular pressure (IOP) associated with glaucoma.

androgen tear – Part of Allergan's technology pipeline for treatment of dry eye.

angiogenesis – The development of blood vessels.

Array – An intraocular lens (IOL) that is designed to match the multiple functions of the accommodative crystalline lens. It uses multifocal refractive zones to provide functional vision at distances near and far, offering surgeons and patients what is hoped to be a new choice in vision correction via cataract surgery.

B

beta blocker – A first-line therapy to treat glaucoma such as Betagan. Betagan suppresses the production of fluid (aqueous humor) in the eye and reduces pressure.

Betagan – A topical ophthalmic nonselective beta-blocker that is used to lower intraocular pressure (IOP) in patients with open-angle glaucoma or ocular hypertension.

Blephamide – A sterile topical ophthalmic ointment combining an antibacterial and a corticosteroid.

blepharitis – Inflammation of the eyelids.

blepharospasm – A twitching or spasmodic contraction of the orbicularis oculi muscle due to habit spasm, eyestrain or nervous twitching.

Blink-N-Clean – A hard lens cleaner used to clean and re-wet contact lenses while they are still in the eye.

Botox – Botulinum Toxin Type A, one of seven serotypes produced by the bacteria Clostridium botulinum. When injected in minute quantities into muscles that are in spasm, Botox can alleviate spasm by inhibiting the release of acetylcholine from nerve endings. Relief from muscle spasms also alleviates pain in many patients.

brimonidine – One of a class of compounds called alpha2 agonists to treat chronic glaucoma. Marketed as Alphagan.

C

cataract – Opacity of the lens of the eye or its capsule or both.

Complete – An all-in-one, soft contact lens solution. It is designed to clean, rinse, disinfect and lubricate.

Conjunctivitis – Inflammation of the mucous membrane that lines eyelids and is reflected onto the eyeball.

Consept F – A preservative-free soft contact lens-care system that Allergan acquired with the purchase of the contact lens-care business of Pilkington Barnes-Hind. It contains three components: Consept 1, a 3 percent hydrogen-peroxide solution with a built-in surfactant cleaner that provides disinfection and cleaning; Consept 2, a neutralizing solution containing sodium thiosulfate; and the HydraMat II, a lens case that washes the lens as you twist the top.

Cortefrin – Allergan's first cortisone ophthalmic product.

cryoprobe – Device used for applying liquid nitrogen to skin tissue.

cervical dystonia – Prolonged muscle contractions in the neck that may cause twisting and repetitive movements or abnormal posture. These movements may be in the form of rhythmic jerks.

E

eczema – Acute or chronic inflammatory condition with scales, scabs or crusts that appear on the skin's surface.

edema – A condition in which the body tissues contain an excessive amount of tissue fluid.

Epifrin – A topical sympathomimetic agent for ophthalmic use.

F

FDA (Food and Drug Administration) – The U.S. Government agency that ensures that all products which are drug or food based are labeled truthfully with the information that people need to use them properly and that the products pass government safety standards.

FML Liquifilm – An ophthalmic steroid indicated for moderate inflammation of the exterior eye. It is used in conditions as varied as allergic conjunctivitis and post-operative inflammation.

G

ganglion cell – Nerve cell bodies that form a mass of nervous tissue that is lying outside the brain or spinal cord.

glaucoma – A group of eye diseases characterized by increase in intraocular pressure (IOP), which results in atrophy of the optic nerve and may result in blindness.

glutamate – A salt from an amino acid formed in the hydrolysis of proteins.

H

Herplex – A metabolic antagonist of the synthesis of DNA. It inhibits the use of thymidic acid. It is used to treat herpes simplex keratitis and vaccinia keratitis.

hypotensive lipid – Derived from prostaglandis, they are a different kind of compound that reduces intraocular pressure (IOP) by improving the outflow of the aqueous humor from the eye.

I

IND – Acronym for Investigational New Drug.

IOL (Intraocular Lens) – A lens implanted to replace the eye's natural lens after it has been removed during cataract surgery.

IOP (Intraocular pressure) – Pressure inside the eye caused by excess fluid entering the eye and/or insufficient fluid draining from the eye.

immune function – The functioning of the immune system to fight off disease and to heal injuries.

in-license – obtaining a license from another company to use their patented or trademarked compound or product.

L

LC – An acronym for lens care.

LC Cleaning Solution – A cleaning solution for contact lens care.

Liquifilm – A topical anti-inflammatory agent for ophthalmic use.

M

MD Forte – Name for a line of Allergan's skin care products recommended mainly by dermatologists. The aesthetic skin care line was acquired from Herald Pharmacal in 1995 and includes facial creams, hand and body lotions and cleansers.

memantine – A glutamate NMDA receptor agonist that protects against glutamate induced retinal ganglion cell death.

N

NDA – An acronym meaning New Drug Application.

neoantergan – An ingredient in allergy medicine.

neuroprotection – An area of research aimed at vision preservation which limits damage caused by increased IOP by focusing on the optic nerve.

neurotoxins – Toxins that attack nerve cells.

O

Ocuflox – A broad spectrum topical anti-infective indicated for the treatment of bacterial conjunctivitis caused by the susceptible strains of Staphylococcus aureus, Staphylococcus pneumoniae, Enterobacter cloacae, Haemophilus influenzae, Proteus mirabilis and Pseudomones aeruginosa.

Oculinum, Inc. – The company that produced Botox. Allergan acquired it in 1991.

open-angle glaucoma – A condition in which the angle between the iris and the cornea is open and in which the outflow blockage occurs in the trabecular meshwork.

out-license – granting a license to another company to use Allergan's patented or trademarked compound or product.

P

Prednefrin – A treatment for eye inflammation. It is the first Allergan product to be marketed nationally.

PVA – An acronym for polyvinyl alcohol.

Propine – A dipivefrin hydrochloride in a sterile, isotonic solution. Dipivefrin hydrochloride is a white, crystalline powder, freely soluble in water.

Phacomoemulsification machine – Allergan's phacoemulsification machines use high frequency ultrasound probes to fragment the cloudednatural lens (cataract) into tiny pieces. The pieces are then gently suctioned out via aspiration. The rim of the anterior capsule and the entire posterior capsule, located between the cornea and the iris, remain intact.

PhRMA – Pharmaceutical Researchers and Manufacturers of America.

psoriasis – A common inflammatory skin condition characterized by frequent episodes of redness, itching, and thick, dry, silvery scales on the skin.

Phaco Flex II – A foldable silicone intraocular lens (IOL) that replaces the eye's natural lens during cataract surgery. The haptics, which secure the lens in place in the patient's eye, are made of extruded PMMA, a biocompatible plastic substance.

prostaglandins – A large group of biologically active, carbon-20, unsaturated fatty acids that represent some of the metabolites of arachidonic acid. Prostaglandin compounds lower intraocular pressure in ocular hypertension and chronic open-angle glaucoma.

R

receptor-selective retinoids – Compounds that have potential applications for treating a variety of diseases, including cancer, eye and skin disorders. Many of these compounds are unique because they have a high degree of receptor sub-type selectivity, meaning they have the potential for increased therapeutic effectiveness while exhibiting reduced side effects.

retinoids – Synthetic analogs of vitamin A. Synthetic analogs include etretinate and isotretinoin. The main use of these compounds is in dermatology.

RARs (Retinoid Acid Receptors) – A compound specific to RAR family. Known to target solid and hematokogic tumors.

RXRs (Retinoid X Receptors) – A compound specific for the retinoid X receptor (RXR) family. RXR agonists may be useful in treating type II diabetes.

Restasis – A cyclosporine ophthalmic emulsion for the treatment of severe dry eye.

S

sulfacetamide – An anti-bacterial sulfonamide that is highly soluable.

steroids – Any of numerous compounds containing a 17-carbon 4-ring system and including the sterols and various hormones and glycosides.

Soflens – An enzymatic contact lens cleaner product.

Sensar – An acrylic IOL for cataract patients.

strambis – Crossed eyes.

Sovereign – A phacoemulsification system that integrates advanced fluidics technology with enhanced power modulations to further reduce risks associated with phacoemulsification procedures.

T

Tazorac – A topical retinoid proven by the USFDA and other federal agencies in treating stable plaque psoriasis on up to 20 percent of the body's surface area. It is a clear, non-greasy, odor-free gel that's safe to use one most parts of the body. It is available in two concentrations, 0.05% and 0.1%.

U

Unfolder, The – A device which allows cataract surgeons the potential for greater intraoperative control through the process of unfolding and implanting three-piece foldable IOLs.

Z

Zorac – The first topical retinoid for the treatment of mild to moderate plaque psoriasis. The key to efficacy and safety of Zorac in treating plaque psoriasis lies in its pharmacological selectivity. Zorac achieves rapid, sustained efficacy by modulating three key pathogenic characteristics of psoriasis-abdominal differentiation, hyperproliferation and inflammation.

INDEX

(**Boldface** type indicates photograph or other image)